Demystify Math, Science, and Technology

Creativity, Innovation, and Problem Solving

Dennis Adams and
Mary Hamm

ROWMAN & LITTLEFIELD EDUCATION
A division of
ROWMAN & LITTLEFIELD PUBLISHERS, INC.
Lanham • *New York* • *Toronto* • *Plymouth, UK*

Published by Rowman & Littlefield Education
A division of Rowman & Littlefield Publishers, Inc.
A wholly owned subsidary of The Rowman & Littlefield Publishing Group, Inc.
4501 Forbes Boulevard, Suite 200, Lanham, Maryland 20706
http://www.rowmaneducation.com

Estover Road, Plymouth PL6 7PY, United Kingdom

British Library Cataloguing in Publication Information Available

Library of Congress Cataloging-in-Publication Data
Adams, Dennis M.
  Demystify math, science, and technology : creativity, innovation, and problem-
solving / Dennis Adams, Mary Hamm.
      p. cm.
  ISBN 978-1-60709-634-4 (cloth : alk. paper)—ISBN 978-1-60709-635-1 (pbk. :
alk. paper)—ISBN 978-1-60709-636-8 (electronic)
  1. Mathematics—Study and teaching (Elementary) 2. Mathematics—Study
and teaching (Middle school) 3. Science—Study and teaching (Elementary) 4.
Science—Study and teaching (Middle school) 5. Technology—Study and teaching
(Elementary) 6. Technology—Study and teaching (Middle school) 7. Group work
in education. I. Hamm, Mary. II. Title.
  QA135.6.A329 2009
  372.7—dc22

                                                                    2009036099

℞ ™ The paper used in this publication meets the minimum requirements of
American National Standard for Information Sciences—Permanence of Paper for
Printed Library Materials, ANSI/NISO Z39.48-1992.

Printed in the United States of America

Contents

Preface

Demystify Math, Science, and Technology provides you with practical and proven processes, tools, and examples that will be useful in applying the principles and strategies of a differentiated math and science curriculum. It assumes that standards-driven math and science instruction can help open doors to creative and innovative thinking. Differentiated instruction and collaborative inquiry are viewed as important features on the path to helping all students learn math and science.

Close attention is also paid to the social nature of learning, and suggestions are given for sparking student interest in open-ended problem solving and collaborative inquiry. *Demystify Math, Science, and Technology* is written in a teacher-friendly style intended to help individual teachers improve their practice. It is organized in a way that is convenient for school districts or universities that are doing in-service work with classroom teachers.

It might also serve as a supplementary text for methods classes in mathematics and science education. Although there are concepts and ideas that apply to any grade, the primary focus is on the elementary and middle school levels. However the book is used, it offers plenty of help and advice for promoting creativity and innovation in the math/science classroom.

We believe that in the evolving local and global economy, the skills related to mathematical problem solving, scientific inquiry, and technology are keys to success in and out of school. Ingenuity, teamwork, and innovative skills are closely related to the intellectual tools of math and science. This whole package of attributes is essential for learners imagining new scenarios and future work in areas that don't even exist yet. Of course, there is the age-old question about whether it is best to teach about innovation and creativity directly or indirectly.

Like many topics, one point of view isn't necessarily true and the other false. It can be both. The difficulty is figuring out *what* is true and *what* is false. You can be sure that innovation will be increasingly important to the success of any developed economy. Another certainty is that the mental discipline needed for sustainable innovation doesn't come about in an educational vacuum.

A major concern here is whether or not the thought processes and logic being propagated by our schools help students change in a way that supports them as they learn how to adjust to a rapidly changing environment. Putting thinking skills at the heart of math and science instruction can help—especially if teachers are able to develop lessons that meet the readiness, interests, and learning profiles of their students.

With such a differentiated approach, support structures, and a high-quality curriculum, both teachers and students will be more able to hold a subject or problem in their minds long enough to see it anew.

An important concern is that many students who are trying to learn about math, science, and their technological associates do not sufficiently connect with these subjects or with their more informed classmates. So, it is little wonder that struggling students don't understand related skills and concepts as well as those who are exploring the more innovative and creative possibilities of math, science, and technology.

In some schools, the intellectual tools and technological products of math and science are being applied in a way that ignites innovative behavior. In others, it is way out beyond the educational horizon.

There are plenty of teachers out there who are more than willing to build problem solving, inquiry, creativity, and innovation into their daily routine. Many are going about doing this by connecting students with engaging and authentic real-world tasks and experiences.

To make this happen, individual teachers must have the tools necessary to go beyond the basics and motivate all learners to be more imaginative and communicative in their approach to math and science. There is now general agreement that encouraging the investigation of the depth and breadth of mathematics and science is better preparation for success in school and in life than a curriculum whose major challenge is how much can be memorized for the short term.

Things like home environment, class size, and school calendar all matter, but nothing is more important than teachers who can work with all the available tools to develop young minds. Part of the math and science teaching problem is that America has not made a reasonable level of investment in teacher education, professional development, and new curricula. Recruiting, training, and keeping good teachers are keys to the academic future of our school systems and the educational competence of the nation.

Experienced educators know that students need to approach learning math and science in different ways. Like more than a few teachers, some learners simply don't like these subjects—and others think they won't be successful. At any level, it seems that poor attitude and poor achievement can amplify each other.

In spite of the challenges, it is possible to appreciate strategies that worked in the past while adapting to today's new realities. Some schools really do it right; the problem is reaching out to all schools across the country.

Regardless of the state of their school system, teachers are increasingly faced with reaching out effectively to students who span the entire spectrum of learning. Student differences include issues surrounding preparedness, personal interests, and cultural ways of seeing and experiencing the world.

We do know that, to build a capacity for student success, you have to identify individual strengths, maximize potential, and build capacity. Although there is no single formula for creating a differentiated classroom, it is our belief that no one should be sidelined with basic skills in a way that keeps them away from the creative and collaborative engagement associated with problem solving, inquiry, and the technological products of math and science.

The following is a suggestion for teachers trying to prepare a math or science lesson for Monday: don't let the pursuit of the long-term perfection stand in the way of goals you can achieve now.

Developing positive attitudes toward math and science goes hand in hand with activating and engaging interest in these subjects. The hope is that the teaching ideas we present will assist teachers as they invite eager *and* reluctant learners to inquire, discover concepts, and collaboratively explore the inter-linking concepts of mathematics, science, and technology. Along the way, students may even acquire the ability to imagine and generate new ideas and collaboratively apply them (a major advantage in today's world).

Technology is a powerful force both in and out of school—and it has long been linked with math and science. Paying attention to this subject also makes sense because mathematicians and scientists rely on technology-supported possibilities as they go about doing their work. The technological products of math and science are important on many levels, so this book pays close attention to the instructional and innovative possibilities of these tools.

Since teachers are the key to educational success, it is important to recognize the fact that they cannot develop the creative and technology-aided innovative abilities of their students if their own abilities in these areas are neglected.

It is our belief that shining a light on mathematical, scientific, and technological processes gives everyone involved more control over everything that is going on around them. We also believe that demystifying practice in the fields of math, science, and technology can help all students gain a better understanding of how things work.

Demystify Math, Science, and Technology recognizes those realities and tries to deepen the collective conversation, challenge thinking, and provide up-to-date tools for teachers so they can help reverse the steady erosion of math and science skills in the general population.

> Education helps a society leverage every other investment it makes, be it in medicine, transportation, or alternative energy.
> It appears to be the best single bet that a society can make.
>
> —D. Leonhardt[1]

1

Creativity, Innovation, and Differentiation

Problem Solving and Inquiry in Math, Science, and Technology

> The future is not the result of choices among alternative paths offered by the present, but a place that is created—created first in mind and will, created next in activity.
>
> —John Schaar[1]

Unless our schools ignite sparks of student creativity in math, science, and technology, Americans may find themselves largely serving as the worldwide information economy's version of manual labor. From the boardroom to the classroom, innovation is seen as the key to a productive future. That future has not been predetermined; it is something that teachers and their students will be involved in creating.

Differentiated instruction (DI) has creativity and innovation built into it because teachers who take that approach are used to making adjustments for students with different learning interests, needs, and fluency. A student or a small group may need more advanced problems, while others may need a hands-on approach that more closely matches their learning style. Mathematical problem solving and scientific inquiry are more natural and effective when students are not served a "one-size-fits-all" path to understanding.

Math, science, and technology questions (or problems) can be designed in a way that nurtures the innovative spirit. A differentiated approach to instruction is guided by the idea that schools should extend individual potential, helping students to grow as much and as quickly as possible. Unlike older individualized learning approaches, differentiated instruction often happens in pairs or in small groups where students take responsibility for

1

what they are doing and help each other master content based on learning goals and curriculum standards.

DI involves recognizing how students' varying backgrounds, knowledge, readiness, and learning preferences affect their work. The next step is making sure that there is some variation in content, process, or product. By *content* we mean multiple paths for taking in information; *process* should allow multiple options for making sense of ideas; and *product* means multiple options for expressing what has been learned.

Clearly, differentiated learning, standards-based instruction, and innovative behavior are compatible with today's math and science classrooms. As far as innovation is concerned, the process begins with creating new ideas in the right environment. Students' attitudes and beliefs are crucial. The basic principles of innovation are *questioning, trusting, taking risks, opening to new ideas,* and *being patient* (Estrin, 2009).

DIFFERENTIATED PROBLEM SOLVING, INQUIRY, AND INNOVATION

DI is built on the belief that students have different needs and that all students can imaginatively approach any subject. Innovation might be thought of as radical or incremental changes in thinking, processes, technologies used, or services. Promoting thinking and innovative skills requires *not* treating students as passive recipients of information. Moving in the most productive direction requires an environment in which students are active learners, decision makers, and problem solvers.

This means that the teacher is often more of a coach or facilitator than a lecturer in front of the class. It is also important to note that even in the most child-centered classroom, the teacher plays an important role by presenting new possibilities for questions and problems.

There is a time and place for individuals to work alone, in pairs, in small groups, and as an entire class. But collaborative discussion is crucial. In a think-pair-share (groups of two) or in small groups of three or four, students can cooperatively work to frame and explore new problems.

Interdependence (sink or swim together) and individual accountability are keys to the success of a small group. By *think-pair-share*, we mean making sure that individual students have a problem or question, asking them to think about it alone for just eight or ten seconds, and then, pairing them up for a discussion. Finally, after a good discussion with the partners, the partnerships share their point of view with the whole class.

At various stages, the teacher might ask "Is there a different way to go about solving it?" or, after time for inquiry, "How would you change things based on what you discovered?" There are times when you may want students to write down their responses. And being ready to gear up (harder) or gear down (simplify) a problem or question is part of what differentiation is about. It is always good to have other questions/problems ready in case there is time to repeat the process.

Although the most important instructional goal of math and science instruction is to understand the content, it is also important for students to learn about the purposes, methods, and innovative behavior associated with these subjects and their technological tools. Teaching students to collaboratively make decisions and complete authentic investigations is part of every lesson plan. A differentiated math/science classroom also provides many opportunities for students to inquire into their own understandings—while learning how to think and work like mathematicians and scientists.

The advance of cognitive learning theories has led educators to realize how important it is for learners to be more actively engaged in their own construction of knowledge. Helping students become efficient problem solvers has long been viewed as an important goal of mathematics instruction. Solving a problem involves finding a way around an obstacle or getting past some difficulty to experience the triumph of discovery.

By engaging in a math-related task before the method of solution becomes clear often results in the development of new knowledge. In the differentiated math classroom, students have frequent opportunities to formulate, work with, and solve complex problems. The process requires a high degree of student effort, and time is needed for reflecting on their own thinking. (There is more to come in chapter 3.)

Both problem solving and inquiry are ways for scientists and students to investigate the world. Although science obviously pays attention to problem solving, inquiry is paramount. Scientific inquiry can be viewed as a process by which questions are asked, evidence is gathered, investigations are carried out, explanations are proposed, and predictions are made. Inquiry is an active problem-solving approach that uses scientific, mathematical, and technological tools to study the natural world and present the results to others.

By taking part in scientific inquiry, students acquire knowledge and develop an understanding of concepts, models, and theories. Inquiry also involves a set of interrelated processes that students and scientists can use to investigate phenomena and creatively think about world situations. Understanding the nature of scientific knowledge, interpreting scientific explanations, and generating/evaluating scientific evidence are all part of the inquiry package. (There is more to come in chapter 4.)

The research tells us that problem solving in math and inquiry in science can motivate and encourage creative and innovative behavior in all types of students (Aleixandre & Erduran, 2008). It also helps learners understand the nature of these subjects and comprehend how they impact their lives.

Math and science education are dynamic fields being influenced by new research findings, national standards, state content requirements, technological advances, the gradual evolution of learning theories, and advances in instructional/assessment strategies. Both subjects integrate technology to encourage creativity and innovative behavior. In spite of all the changes and disagreements, attending to problem solving in math and teaching science as inquiry is supported by all the major stakeholders.

Problem solving, inquiry, and creative reasoning sometimes include students' questioning conventional wisdom and seeking out evidence to support their arguments. It is just as important to get students to go beyond old and new facts to discover new ways to think about them. Innovative ideas can be generated by encouraging a diversity of thinking when students are engaged in authentic performance tasks that require both self-expression and content mastery. It also helps if teachers set up time and space for reflection, experimentation, and the collaborative generation of new ideas.

Regardless of the math or science lesson, students must develop certain habits of the mind, employ critical reasoning skills, and productively participate in the process. Clearly, in the differentiated classroom, problem solving, inquiry, and innovation are natural allies (Bass, Contant, & Carin, 2009).

Math and science courses temper the human spirit, refine it, and make it a tool with which one may creatively tackle any kind of material.

—Francis Perkins[2]

BASIC PRINCIPLES OF INNOVATION

Innovation has a lot to do with the creation of new ideas, approaches, or things. It might also involve transforming an idea or invention into a problem-solving device, process, product, or technique. Uniqueness and novelty are key criteria.

Innovation requires *questioning*. Questioning provides room to explore. To explore is to discover new ideas. Questions can be inquisitive or judgmental. Discovering questions convey interest. Questions such as "Can you explain . . ." are open-ended assumptions or hypotheses found in mathematical problem solving and scientific inquiry. Teaching through inquiry can provide students with many questions. They are yearning to explore them. Students take innovative steps in authentic investigation and problem solving.

Questioning and inquiry promote active learning in the differentiated classroom. Questions like "Why did you . . ." express judgment, not confidence, faith, or trust. Students can continue to question their assumptions and pursue bold, broad-ranging innovation.

Trusting is another principle of innovation. As a teacher, you need to trust your students, and students need to trust themselves, the teacher, and each other. Trust happens when students understand that the teacher is there to support them. Teachers in differentiated classrooms often use small group instruction, personalized learning assignments, independent studies, learning contracts, open discussions, and many other strategies to make learning work for each student.

Teachers honor student voices by inviting student ideas, encouraging student thoughts, and affirming, supporting, and responding with honesty. Part of trusting is seen as being fair. Trusting yourself and others is necessary for success.

Risking means taking a chance. Failure is part of risk taking and a part of innovation. Accepting failure is not easy and often painful. Being able to give up what we passionately believe requires tolerance and patience. Our aim is for accountability without blame. An element of risk ("Is it going to work, or not?") adds excitement. The eagerness to take bold, yet calculated risks is one of the basic principles of innovation.

Opening to new ideas is another basic principle of innovation. It requires an open mind and an open atmosphere where everyone is encouraged to imagine, think broadly, and collaborate on essential questions. Openness captures serendipity and gives learners the freedom to create. Part of openness involves a type of curiosity that stimulates the ability to critically evaluate data, accept input, and be ready to adapt to change.

Stimulating the imagination matters because without it innovation is stifled and independent self-expression and standards mastery are diminished. Being open to surprise and openly sharing information creates avenues for valuable feedback. Once a pair or small group of students agrees on a problem and path of inquiry, the next step is executing a plan and opening their minds to the possibilities.

Being patient is mandatory if innovation is to succeed. Having patience allows ideas to ripen. Innovators need to be able to endure uncertainty, to doubt and wait, instead of jumping at the first solution that comes along. They must have the strength to overcome obstacles and to defend their daring ideas. Time frames and appropriate measurement techniques help calculate how well you are doing. There are times when you can't tell whether something is going to succeed. Teachers can't have someone looking over their shoulder saying, "How are you doing?"

There is not a predictable path to successful innovation. Historically, half of the great innovations arise from extraordinary insights; the other half had more to do with chance. Whether it was inspired insight or blind luck, academic preparation, circumstance, location, and openness to new experiences had a lot to do with it.

DI requires that teachers know their students and make learning personally relevant for them. Knowing your students opens many doors to academic success. The teacher must comprehend what each student knows and can accomplish at a certain time in order to plan and alter instruction in a way that keeps students on task. In fact, DI stands or falls based largely on the teacher's ability to monitor students' nearness to content goals throughout the learning cycle. Of course, success or failure is not just the teacher's responsibility; it's up to the students to develop the ability and the inclination to monitor their progress toward goal attainment.

Armed with assessment information and knowledge of the students, teachers can adapt their teaching plans to ensure student readiness, interest, and individual learning styles. Once teachers know what students understand, what they can or cannot do, and what motivates them to learn, they can try to make sure that students attain an understanding of basic information. Teachers can also help students take charge of their learning and take charge of their lives.

DIFFERENTIATION: ONE SIZE DOESN'T FIT ALL

Making sure that the learning is tailored to each student is another part of promoting creativity and innovation in the classroom. Asking students to do what they are ready to do avoids a lot of aggravation for everybody. If work is too easy, it can prevent them from addressing the challenge. If it's too hard, frustration and bad attitude set in. In either case, the students' willingness to continue when they face difficulty with math, science, or technology vanishes. Remember, it's just as bad to say that Jane is bored as it is to say that Johnny can't count.

Matching student learning with what they care about always helps. When students know they can do the task and care about it, they will most likely do whatever it takes to succeed. This implies that students can express their learning in ways that will help them succeed. Many discouraged students think they can't complete the assignments. Meeting students where they are in their academic achievement, interests, and preferred learning styles allows teachers to help students reflect on their feelings of failure.

To counteract these negative impressions and connect with their world, it's helpful to use graphic novels and images from the Internet that reflect their feelings about math, science, reading, and technology.

Teachers in differentiated classrooms use small group instruction, reading partnerships, text at different reading levels, independent studies, varied homework assignments, and personalized evaluations. Teachers are flexible with work time making learning apply for each student. They use ongoing formative assessment practices, connecting the latest information to curriculum instruction and DI. They constantly study their students to understand what they need and adjust their teaching.

POWER OVER LEARNING

Letting students make responsible decisions on how to use their time is one way to give students some power over their learning. Teachers respect student ideas by inviting their opinions, encouraging participation, and being honest (Tomlinson, Brimijoin, & Narvaez, 2008). Because differentiated learning promotes individualization, teachers can effectively respond to student needs and communicate in a nurturing way. Differentiated teachers make time for student discussions, help solve problems with small groups, ask for student input in developing classroom rules, and provide opportunities for students to review each other's work.

Trust and making sure that students understand what they can do are intertwined with empowerment. They are attempting to meet the broad needs, backgrounds, and learning styles of a diverse student population. Today, we know much more about why some students have little trouble learning and others struggle. We know the value of a student's preparedness, learning style, interests, and confidence in learning.

As schools are adapting to an increasingly broad range of learners, it is more important than ever to design math, science, and technology instruction in ways that accommodate academically diverse learners. DI can be part of the answer. With a standards-based curriculum in place in almost every state, all students are expected to achieve at high levels. In the past, there was a group of students who ended up being placed in low-achieving classes. Now, we must find ways to make higher achievement available for everyone.

DI is a collection of approaches that help you direct and manage the variety of learning needs in your classroom. DI that fosters innovation depends on how you identify your students' learning needs effectively and how you offer learning opportunities that increase the probability of student success. DI is a proven way to ensure that fewer children are left behind and that higher levels of attainment are reached.

Teachers have always had to deal with the fact that individual students learn things in different ways. And most realize that schools are places where teachers learn from students and students can learn from each other. Although differentiated math/science/technology instruction is a more recent development, it is an easy fit for many teachers.

DI is nothing new. It is based on the best practices in education. It puts students at the center of learning. It allows their learning needs to help you manage your instructional planning. The first step in differentiated learning is to begin where you are. Differentiation does not mean throwing out your planning from past years. It means analyzing how well you're providing variety and challenge in learning, recognizing which students are best served by your current plans, and altering those plans as needed so more students can be successful.

LEARNING GOALS OF DIFFERENTIATION

Differentiated learning helps students not only master content but also shape their learning identities. DI increases learning for all students by involving them in activities that respond to their individual needs, strengths, and inclinations. Differentiated goals include the following:

- Developing challenging and engaging tasks for every learner
- Creating instructional activities based on the necessary topics, concepts, and skills of math, science, and technology, and providing ways for students to display what they have learned
- Offering flexible approaches to content and instruction
- Paying attention to students' readiness, instructional needs, and learning preferences
- Meeting curriculum standards for each learner

Differentiated innovation involves adapting instruction to meet the needs of students with a wide range of needs and academic abilities. It involves recognizing the fact that individuals and small clusters of students can use different content, processes, and products to achieve the same conceptual understanding.

Differentiated responses from the teacher can be as simple as rephrasing a question—or as complicated as regrouping on the basis of student interests. DI is much more than individualized learning or designing a lesson for every student. It involves building mixed-ability group instruction around the idea that individual students (or groups of students) learn in unique ways and at varying levels of difficulty. Assessment can follow a similar path. And along with teacher observation, it can influence grouping decisions.

What children can do together today they can do alone tomorrow.

—Vygotsky[3]

A good way for learning groups to connect with DI is for teachers to base group assignments on what they know about the interests and aptitudes of the students involved. In addition, there are times when students may need multiple chances to demonstrate mastery. In a differentiated classroom, you will find students doing more thinking for themselves *and* working more with peers.

Self-evaluation and a gentle kind of peer assessment are both part of the process. With DI, small collaborative groups within the class are often working at different levels of complexity and at different rates. Math, science, and technology lessons can be differentiated based on a students' interest in these subjects, readiness to learn a concept, and their preferred path to comprehension.

Language makes us human
Art and culture push the boundaries of human understanding
Science and its mathematical tools help us understand the natural world
Technology makes us powerful
And being in community with others makes us free.

—Dennis Adams

ELEMENTS THAT GUIDE DIFFERENTIATED LEARNING

The *content* that teachers teach and how students have access to information are important ways for teachers to differentiate instruction. Curriculum content is often determined by the school or district and reflects state or national standards. You differentiate content when you preassess students' skills and knowledge, then *match students with activities according to their readiness.* Student readiness is the current knowledge understanding and skill level of a student. Readiness does not mean student ability; rather, it reflects what a student knows, understands, and is able to do.

Interest is another way to differentiate learning. Topics students enjoy learning about, thinking about, and doing provide a motivating link. Successful teachers incorporate required content to students' interests to engage the learner. This helps students connect with new information by making it appealing, relevant, and worthwhile.

A student's *learning profile* is influenced by an individual's preferred learning style, "intelligence" preference, academic interests, and cultural background. By tapping into a student's learning profile, teachers can extend the ways students learn best.

A *differentiated learning environment* enables teachers and students to work in ways that benefit each student and the class as a whole. A flexible environment allows students to make decisions about how to make the classroom surroundings work. This gives students a feeling of ownership and a sense of responsibility. Students of any age can work successfully as long as they know what's expected and are held to high standards of performance.

IMPORTANT PRINCIPLES OF DIFFERENTIATION

Several key principles describe a differentiated classroom. A few of them are defined here:

- A *high-quality engaging curriculum* is the beginning principle. Your first job as a teacher is to guarantee that the curriculum is consistent, inviting, important, and thoughtful.
- Students' work should be appealing, inviting, thought provoking, and stimulating. *Every student should find his or her work interesting and powerful.*
- Teachers should try to *assign challenging tasks* that are a little too difficult for the student. Be sure there is a support system to assist students' success at a level they never thought possible.
- *Use adjustable grouping.* It is important for you to plan times for groups of students to work together—and times for students to work independently. Provide teacher-choice and student-choice groups.
- *Assessment is a formative ongoing process.* Teachers often preassess students to determine students' knowledge and skills based on their needs. Once you are aware of what students already know and what they need to learn, then you can differentiate instruction to match the needs of each student. Formative assessment allows teachers to alter instruction while learning is going on.
- When it comes to planning activities or assignments, we often use a *tiered approach.* Tiered methods are differentiated learning ways to teach that you develop based on your diagnosis of students' needs. When you use a tiered approach, you are prescribing individual techniques to particular groups of students. Within each group, you decide whether students do assignments alone, with a partner, or as a collaborative learning team.

The basic idea is to have a wide range of students learn the concept being taught. But students can reach competency in many different ways. The first step is to identify the key skills and concepts that everyone must understand. All students in a class cover the same topic, but the teacher varies materials based on students' aptitudes and interests.

- *At least some grades should be based on growth.* A struggling student who persists and doesn't see progress will likely become frustrated if grade-level benchmarks seem out of his or her reach and growth doesn't appear to count. It is your job to support the student by making sure (one way or another) the student masters the concepts required. When it's time for final assessments, it's important to plan several assessment strategies—for example, a quiz and a project.

When it comes to DI, teachers need to realize that differentiation is about grouping according to the social, academic, interests, and emotional needs of students. It's not about ability grouping. Teachers need the ability to build motivating lessons for mixed-ability groups. And they need to think about their craft as they practice it. Better thinking also requires paying at least some attention to connecting theory and research to practice. If students have trouble learning math and science from the way we teach, then we need to pay attention to their personal resources and teach them in a way they can learn.

MULTIPLE INTELLIGENCES: ANOTHER PART OF DIFFERENTIATED INSTRUCTION

The goal of DI is to increase the chances that students will be successful learners. A way to achieve this is to get to know students and to understand how they differ in interests, learning preferences, readiness, and motivation. It is necessary for teachers to realize that students learn and create in different ways. Although we know it is often best to teach to students' strengths, providing them with deep learning experiences in different domains can also enrich their "intelligence" in specific areas.

Carol Tomlinson's idea of the differentiated classroom is based, in part on the work of Howard Gardner and Robert Sternberg. They contributed to the awareness that students exhibit different intelligence preferences. Gardner projected that intelligence could be thought of as a variety of independent intelligences rather than an overall measure of mental ability. He identified eight intelligences that represent different ways a child may understand or explain their knowledge. These include the following:

Linguistic: the ability to use language to express ideas.
Logical/mathematical: the ability to explore patterns and relationships by manipulating objects or symbols in an orderly manner.
Musical: the capacity to think in music; the ability to perform, compose, or enjoy a musical piece.
Spatial: the ability to understand and mentally manipulate a form or object in a visual or spatial display.
Bodily-kinesthetic: the ability to move your body through space and use motor skills in sports, performing arts, or art productions (particularly dance or acting).

Interpersonal: the ability to work in groups; interacting, sharing, leading, following, and reaching out to others.

Intrapersonal: the ability to understand your inner feelings, dreams, and ideas.

Naturalist: the ability to discriminate among living things (plants and animals) as well as sensitivity to the natural world.

Sternberg suggests three intelligence preferences:

Analytic (schoolhouse intelligence)
Creative (imaginative intelligence)
Practical (contextual, street-smart intelligence)

Today, there is still discussion about what these intelligences represent or if there are additional intelligences. Our purpose here is to develop a broad collection of instructional activities that offer learning choices for each of the intelligences. You may wish to use these intelligences as paths for learning.

Students have a range of strengths and weaknesses, and the effective teacher can put into action lessons that provide learning activities that speak to a wide assortment of these intelligences. By doing so, the teacher can provide the best learning opportunities for students who have different strengths in each intelligence. Teachers are also encouraged to plan their lesson activities with these intelligences in mind.

Gardner's work can help you add excitement to the ways you teach and the projects you assign. It can also help you find out more about your students, the ways they learn best and what they like to do. The activities in this book look at student activities using DI. We explain what differentiation would look like and sound like in the classroom.

ACTIVITIES THAT REFLECT
THE MULTIPLE INTELLIGENCE THEORY

1. Upper elementary and middle school students can comprehend the Multiple Intelligence (MI) Theory. One way to discover students' interests and strengths is to explain the MI Theory to them and provide them with a list of possible activities.
2. Ask your students to review the MI activities list and note which ones they choose the most. Make sure your students understand the purpose of this activity is to find out students' learning strengths.

STUDENT ACTIONS: USING DIRECT INSTRUCTION

Read the lists and underline all the MI activities you enjoy doing, presenting, or performing. Here are some possibilities:

linguistic intelligence

writing an article
developing a newscast
making a plan, describing a procedure
writing a letter
writing a play
interpreting a text or a piece of writing
conducting an interview
debating

musical intelligence

singing a rap song
giving a musical presentation
explaining music similarities
demonstrating rhythmic patterns
performing music

logical-mathematical intelligence

designing and conducting an experiment
describing patterns
making up analogies to explain
solving a problem
inventing a code
designing a website

spatial intelligence

illustrating, sketching
creating a slideshow
    chart, map, or graph
creating a piece of art
drawing, painting, videotaping

bodily-kinesthetic intelligence

using creative movement
designing task or puzzle cards
building or constructing something
bringing materials to demonstrate
using technology to explain something
using the body to persuade or support

interpersonal intelligence

participating in a service project
conducting a meeting
teaching someone
consoling others
advising a friend or fictional
    character others

naturalist intelligence

preparing an observation notebook
describing changes in the environment
caring for pets, wildlife, gardens, or parks
using binoculars, telescopes, or
    microscopes
photographing natural objects

intrapersonal intelligence

writing a journal entry
describing one of your values
assessing your work
setting and pursuing a goal
reflecting on emotions
dreaming

analytic   *creative*
reviewing basic skills   imagining, creating

contextual
being street smart

3. Once students have expressed their choices, have them do some activities to help them remember the intelligences. We like having students
   work with a partner and create activities.
4. Introduce various learning styles:

   Mastery style learner—concrete learner, step-by-step process; learns
      sequentially.
   Understanding style learner—focuses on ideas and abstractions; learns
      through a process of questioning.
   Self-expressive style learner—looks for images; uses feelings and emo-
      tions
   Interpersonal style learner—focuses on the concrete, prefers to learn
      socially, and judges learning in terms of its potential use in helping
      others.

   Encourage students to identify their preferred learning style and get
   together with their team to review learning preferences.

5. Build on students' interests.

   When students do research either individually or with a group, allow
   them to choose a project that appeals to them. Students should also
   choose the best way for communicating their understanding of the
   topic. In this way, students discover more about their interests, concerns, learning styles, and intelligences.

6. Plan interesting lessons. There are many ways to plan interesting lessons.

   Lesson plan ideas presented here are influenced by ideas as diverse as
   those of John Goodlad, Madeline Hunter, and Howard Gardner.

LESSON PLANNING

1. Set the tone of the lesson. Focus student attention, relate the lesson to
   what students have done before. Stimulate interest.
2. Present the objectives and purpose of the lesson. What are students
   supposed to learn? Why is it important?

3. Provide background information: what information is available? Resources such as books, journals, videos, pictures, maps, charts, teacher lectures, class discussions, or seat work may be listed.
4. Define procedures: what are students supposed to do? This includes examples and demonstrations as well as working directions.
5. Monitor students' understanding. During the lesson, the teacher may check students' understanding and adjust the lesson if necessary. Teachers invite questions and ask for clarification. A continuous feedback process is always in place.
6. Provide guided practice experiences where students have a chance to use the new knowledge presented under direct teacher supervision.
7. Offer students many opportunities for independent practice where they can use their new knowledge and skills.
8. Evaluate and assess students' work to show that students have demonstrated an understanding of important concepts.
9. Lesson plan formats are included in the resources list.

A SAMPLE MULTIPLE INTELLIGENCE LESSON PLAN

Differentiated Brain Lesson: How Neurons Work

The basic idea is to develop understanding of personal health, changes in environments, and local challenges in science and technology. The human body and the brain are fascinating areas of study. The brain, like the rest of the body, is composed of cells; but brain cells are different from other cells. Neurons grow and develop when they are used actively, and they diminish when they are not used.

All students must be involved in vigorous new learning or they risk losing brain power. High interest/low vocabulary materials such as colorful charts are desirable when teaching new concepts to struggling learners. A chart of a neuron of the brain including cell body, dendrite, and axon is a helpful teaching tool when introducing this concept.

This lesson focuses on the math standards of problem solving, estimation, data analysis, logic, reasoning, communication, and math computations. The science standards of inquiry, life science, science and technology, and personal and social perspectives are also part of the lesson.

Lesson Goals

The basic goal is to provide a dynamic experience with each of the eight "intelligences" and map out a chart on construction paper.

Procedures

1. Divide the class into groups. Assign each group an intelligence.
2. Allow students time to prepare an activity that addresses their intelligence. Each small group will give a three-minute presentation (with a large map) to the entire class. Let reluctant students see, hear, touch, and write about new or difficult concepts. Utilize materials that assess present learner needs. Allow the class to develop their own problems.

Objective

To introduce students to the terminology of the brain and how the brain functions, specifically the functions of the neurons.

Grade Level

With modifications, K–8.

Materials

Paper, pens, markers, copy of a picture of the brain, the neuron, songs about the brain, and model of the brain (recipe follows).

Brain "Recipe"

Pour five cups of instant potato flakes, five cups of hot water, and two cups of sand into a one-gallon zip lock bag.

Combine all ingredients; mix thoroughly. It should weigh about three pounds and have a consistency of a real brain.

Background Information

No one understands exactly how the brain works. But scientists know the answer lies within the billions of tiny cells, called *neurons* or nerve cells, that make up the brain. All the body's feelings and thoughts are caused by the electrical and chemical signals passing from one neuron to the next. A neuron looks like a tiny octopus but with many more tentacles (some have several thousand). Neurons carry signals throughout the brain that allows the brain to move, hear, see, taste, smell, remember, feel, and think.

Procedure

1. Make a model of the brain to show to the class. The teacher displays the brain and says, "The smell of a flower, the memory of a walk in

the park, the pain of stepping on a nail—these experiences are made possible by the three pounds of tissue in our heads—"THE BRAIN!"
2. Show a picture of the neuron and mention its various parts.
3. Have the students label the parts of the neuron and color them, if desired.

Activity 1—Message Transmission: Explaining How the Nerve Cells (Neurons) Work

A message traveling in the nervous system of the brain can go two hundred miles per hour. These signals are transmitted from neuron to neuron across synapses.

1. Instruct students to get into groups of five. Each group should choose a group leader. Include all students, even those who seem not interested.
2. Direct students to stand up and form a circle. Each person is going to be a neuron. Students should be an arm's length away from the next person.
3. When the group leader says "Go," have one person from the group start the signal transmission by slapping the hand of the adjacent person. The second person then slaps the hand of the next, and so on until the signal goes all the way around the circle and the transmission is complete. Utilize materials that address learners' needs. Allow the entire class to become involved in this learning exercise. This helps underachieving learners realize they can work successfully and have fun with peers.

Explanation

The hand that receives the slap is the "dendrite." The middle part of the student's body is the "cell body." The arm that gives the slap to the next person is the "axon," and the hand that gives the slap is the "nerve terminal." In between the hands of two people is the "synapse."

Inquiry Questions

As the activity progresses, questions will arise such as "What are parts of a neuron?" A neuron is a tiny nerve cell, one of billions that make up the brain. A neuron has three basic parts—*the cell body, the dendrites,* and the *axon.* Have students make a simple model by using their hand and spreading their fingers wide. The hand represents the "cell body," the fingers represent "dendrites" that bring information to the cell body, and the arm represents the "axon" that takes information away from the cell body. Just as students wiggle their fingers, the dendrites are constantly moving as they seek information.

If the neuron needs to send a message to another neuron, the message is sent out through the axon. The wrist and forearm represent the axon. When a neuron sends information down its axon to communicate with another neuron, it never actually touches the other neuron. The message goes from the axon of the sending neuron by "swimming" through the space called the synapse. Neuroscientists define *learning* as *two neurons communicating with each other.* They say neurons have "learned" when one neuron sends a message to another neuron (Hannaford, 2005).

Activity 2—Connect the Dots

This exercise is used to illustrate the complexity of the connections of the brain.

1. Have students draw ten dots on one side of a sheet of typing paper and ten dots on the other side of the paper.
2. Tell students to imagine these dots represent neurons; assume each neuron makes connections with the ten dots on the other side.
3. Then connect each dot on one side with the dots on the other side. This is quite a simplification. Each neuron (dot) may actually make thousands of connections with other neurons.

Another part of the activity is teaching brain songs to students: Teach a small group of students the words and the melody of the songs. Include struggling students in this song process. They will become the brain song "experts."

"I've Been Working on My Neurons" (Sung to the tune "I've Been Working on the Railroad")

I've been working on my neurons, all the livelong day.
I've been working on my neurons, Just to make my dendrites play.
Can't you hear the synapse snapping? Impulses bouncing to and fro,
Can't you tell that I've been learning? See how much I know!

"Because I Have a Brain" (Sung to the tune "If I Only Had a Brain" from the movie Wizard of Oz)

I can flex a muscle tightly, or tap my finger lightly,
It's because I have a brain,

I can swim in the river, though it's cold and makes me shiver,
Just because I have a brain.
I am really fascinated, to be coordinated,
It's because I have a brain.
I can see lots of faces, feel the pain of wearing braces,
Just because I have a brain.
Oh, I appreciate the many things that I can do.
I can taste a chicken stew, or smell perfume, or touch the dew.
I am heavy with emotion, and often have the notion,
That life is never plain.
I have lots of personality, a sense of true reality,
Because I have a brain.

Activity 3—Introduce Graphic Organizers

Graphic organizers help students remember information. Mind mapping or webbing shows the main idea and supporting details. To make a mind map, write an idea or concept in the middle of a sheet of paper. Draw a circle around it. Then draw a line from the circle. Write a word or phrase to describe the concept. Draw other lines coming from the circle. Then have students draw pictures to represent their descriptions. Students can start mapping by examining the skill section of their map. Encourage students to talk about word choices and their picture creations.

Activity 4—Review the Physical Science Principles of Matter

The beginning activities on principles of matter shown here help students reveal their exciting curiosity as they observe, manipulate, and sort common objects and materials in their environment. They continue to explain their ideas of the world as they work with the National Science Education Standards.

Science Standards on the Principles of Matter

Children should be aware of the following:

- the properties of objects and materials (K–4)
- the way properties of matter change (5–8)

Ideas and Principles that Help Explain the National Science Standards

- Many things in the natural world can be observed (K–4).
- Natural things are made of many materials (5–8).

- Properties are often used to sort or group objects or materials (K–4).
- Materials come in different forms—solids, liquids, and gases (K–4).

Properties of Objects and Materials.   Material objects are described by their distinctive properties. Students investigate and classify objects in many different ways. Some objectives follow:

- describing characteristics of objects as something that you can see, hear, smell, touch, or taste
- creating ways to describe and sort objects based on their properties
- using descriptions and classifications to show important characteristics of objects such as balls and buttons

Materials for each group follow:

- a variety of different buttons
- one tray to hold the buttons being observed

How Buttons Are the Same and Different

Engage: With children in a large group, present an object like a ball. Ask students to tell what they know about the object. Using their senses can they describe it? What is its shape and color, and what does it feel like? Then, have them look at a large button. Have them use their senses to observe it. In their groups, have them make observations and play a game with lots of buttons.

Explore: Organize children into collaborative groups. Each small group gets about fifteen different buttons on a tray. Have children observe the buttons and describe them to each other. A child describes the button's shape, color, and other properties like the number of holes it has.

Explain: As a class, ask "What words can you use to describe the buttons you observed?" Tell students the scientific word used to describe objects is *property*. A property refers to a characteristic of an object that can be observed with your senses. Review other uses of the word *property* with the students; emphasize its use in science.

Questioning: What are buttons used for? How do they work?

Evaluate: Have students select a button. Write as many words as you can to describe its properties.

SCIENCE AND MATH INNOVATIVE ACTIVITIES

The activities presented here, unless otherwise specified, are designed for elementary students. The following activity was planned with elementary students in mind, but with creativity, the techniques can be adapted for middle school learners.

1. To Observe and Describe Using the Five Senses

Description

This primary activity uses the five senses. The process skills of observing, inferring, communicating (sharing), and hypothesizing are introduced.

Planning Group

Members should arrange the classroom and materials.

Objectives

1. Students will observe and make inferences with their senses.
2. Students will talk and share their ideas with others.
3. Students will ask questions and make hypotheses based on their senses.
4. Struggling students will verify their thinking through personal experiences.

Procedures

1. Select several objects that are safe to touch, smell, and taste (cookies, orange, apple, and popcorn are good choices).
2. Put one object in a clean paper bag, and ask students to feel the object without looking inside.
3. Have students describe what they feel.
4. Have students smell the object without peeking.
5. Encourage students to describe what they smell.
6. Shake the bag, and invite students to describe what they hear.
7. Next, you may wish to have students taste the object and describe it.
8. Finally, allow students to look at the object and verify their guesses.

It's important to discuss with students the strategies they used in making their guesses. Point out the invaluable role of others. Ask what they learned from other classmates about making inferences. Experiences in inferring and describing give students an opportunity to develop and refine many science and math concepts.

Students may use vague or emotional terms rather than specific descriptive words. It's important to discuss the communication process, wherein words are most effective in describing what they did. Let students discuss which words give better descriptions. Have students relate their everyday language to math and science language and symbols. The following activity gives struggling students a chance to refine their skills.

Evaluation

Have students share their experiences through language and cultural anecdotes.

Language materials designed to teach non-English-speaking students are valuable when helping the struggling student.

2. What Do You See?

Description: Grades 3–4

This group center activity involves the process skills of observing, inferring, measuring, comparing, and recording.

Objectives

1. Students will be able to observe and record data accurately.
2. Students will use simple scientific equipment.
3. Students will demonstrate the ability to work in groups in an organized and productive manner.

Process Skills

Measuring, comparing, inferring, ordering by distance, formulating conclusions.

Planning Group

Members should arrange the classroom and materials.

Materials

1. Five samples: a house fly, a computer disk, a flower, a piece of fabric, and a sample of paper. (Other samples may be substituted for those listed.)
2. Twelve magnifying glasses.
3. Six rulers.
4. An observation sheet for each student.

Procedure

1. Six stations, each including two magnifying glasses, one of the samples listed above, and a ruler, are set up around the room.

2. Each student receives an observation sheet.
3. Students are divided into six groups of four students each.
4. Each group is assigned a station. At this station, the group has ten minutes to record as many observations about the sample as possible.
5. Each student in the group, while using the magnifying glass and the ruler, makes an observation for the group to record. Students take turns as time allows.
6. As a class, students compare and discuss their observations.
7. Struggling students are actively involved whether they're the group leader or just part of the team. If students have difficulty, encourage them to work together as a partnership.

Evaluation

Data sheets are evaluated on organization, observation skills, and accuracy.

DI is a proven path to principles that can guide instruction; it provides a useful vehicle for teachers who want to modify or adapt math, science, or technology content.

CONSTRUCTING UNDERSTANDING IN A DIFFERENTIATED CLASSROOM

The rapid advance of cognitive learning theories helped educators realize the need for students to be more actively involved in their own construction of knowledge. Science and its mathematical and technological tools have a lot to tell us about the future. Literature lets us in on other possibilities— and it helps us understand who we are.

Good stories have a lot to offer every subject. Unfortunately, many stories that connect to math or science simply tell children and young adults what mathematicians and scientists have found out about certain phenomena. Too many books leave out the drama of discovery and the trial/error work it took to solve a problem. Still, teachers can build on just about any story with a differentiated mixture of problem solving, inquiry, discussion, and a little extra detail.

Successful differentiated classrooms are full of energy, excitement, and the possibility of teaching all students no matter what learning modality they prefer. Learning math and science is a process that is different for each student. In addition to individual aptitudes, teamwork skills and having a positive attitude matter.

So, it is little wonder that many educators find DI useful in moving students with a variety of academic strengths in the direction of viewing education as the way to light up their future. With all the positive possibilities, teachers are coming to view DI as an important ally in meeting the needs of students with increasingly diverse levels of prior knowledge, interests, and cultural backgrounds.

DI is responsive to specific individual and small group needs—as well as to class performance as a whole. By preparing lessons that differentiate learning, teachers can meet the needs of every student in today's diverse classrooms. It has proven to be a solid asset for teachers trying to reach students who are performing at varying levels in science and math.

DI is an organized, yet flexible, way of adjusting teaching and learning to meet students where they are and helping them accomplish more academically. By creating a differentiated classroom, teachers can do a better job of helping students become self-reliant and motivated learners. Clearly, it is a good way to meet both individual and group needs in the regular classroom.

Since students don't all learn at the same rate, it is important to consider the pacing of math, science, and technology instruction when figuring out the differentiated options. While building on group cooperation, you can provide different individual paths for learning math and science. When it comes to innovation, there is real power in coupling teamwork with individual accountability.

By having the opportunity to collaboratively explore ideas, even unmotivated students tend to respond to appropriate challenges and enjoy learning about science and math. Flexible grouping and pacing, tiered assignments, performance assessment, and other factors associated with DI can inject fresh energy into math, science, and technology instruction.

Teachers often find that it is a good idea to make sure students have access to more good ideas and problems than they can work on. This leaves more room for choice and serendipity; the ideas that have been set aside can inspire students to creatively rethink whatever it is they are focusing on. In a differentiated classroom, teachers often encourage students to bring ideas forward without fear of premature evaluation. Not every idea is good, but when students feel they aren't being listened to, they tend to go silent.

Students' personal interests, learning profiles, and curiosity about a specific topic or skill are major considerations in differentiated problem-solving and inquiry activities. An added advantage to such an approach is that teachers often report that they enjoy teaching more (Sutman, Schmuckler, & Woodfield, 2008).

SUMMARY AND CONCLUSION

In school and in life, it is not always what you know that counts but rather how rapidly you can learn and if you can make good use of your imagination. Innovation is not magic and there really are ways to increase the odds that it will happen. Asking the right questions and dealing with things that are hard to predict (ambiguity) is a part of innovative behavior.

In the differentiated math and science classroom, it certainly helps when teachers encourage a diversity of creative approaches that foster connection and conversation. Although it may be possible to get at these skills directly, it is often better to integrate them into the context of mathematical and scientific situations so that students see the relevancy of what they are learning.

Teachers and students can profit by looking for specific problems and inquiry paths that are likely to prompt certain intellectual tools—allowing for the development of certain mathematical, scientific, and technology-connected ideas. Clearly, it is important for schools to encourage thinking skills and the kind of intelligence behavior needed to approach predictable and unpredictable problems.

And it is usually important for students to efficiently finish what they start. But they need to know that there are times when an unsolvable problem simply gets left behind and fades into irrelevancy. At other times, 80 percent of a problem can be solved—and it isn't worth the time or trouble to deal with the remaining 20 percent. Tenacity is a key to success, but obsession dissipates productive energy.

When it comes to promoting creativity and innovation, working smarter can be better than working harder. Also, multiple experiences in different contexts, at different levels of complexity, seem to lend themselves to the development of an innovative spirit (Michalewicz & Michalewicz, 2008). Creativity and innovation can also be fostered by encouraging students to express themselves using multiple media—especially when learners engage in tasks that require open-ended problem solving, collaborative inquiry, and the application of reasoning skills.

Some of the intellectual tools that support innovative mathematicians and scientists as they go about investigating the world are also appropriate for children and young adults. In addition, mathematical problem solving and scientific inquiry can motivate and encourage all types of students to ask thoughtful questions. The learning of math and science is further amplified when students comprehend the nature of these subjects and their relevance to their lives.

This is helped along the way when students learn how to connect prior knowledge to observations and use evidence to increase their personal knowledge of how the world works. Differentiation comes into play because abilities related to problem solving, inquiry, and innovative approaches develop over time and at different rates.

How do we make sure that schools build the investigative skills and the inventive habits of the mind associated with math and science into the daily classroom routine? Experience has shown that widespread changes in curriculum and instruction are most successful where there are good relationships among teachers, principals, and parents. Local school districts, policy makers, and professional associations are natural allies in the effort to differentiate and improve math and science instruction.

But sometimes teachers have to proceed on their own. Rather than waiting for a compelling vision from on high, many educators have to write and make the final edit of their own narrative. Teachers have always been able to do a lot on their own, but systemic restructuring is easier and more sustainable when there is an arrangement for consultation between the major stakeholders.

> The future is not some place we are going to, but one we are creating. The paths are not to be found, but made, and the activity then changes both the maker and the destination.
>
> —John Schaar

REFERENCES

Aleixandre, M., & Erduran, S. (2008). *Argumentation in science education: Perspectives from classroom-based research.* Dordrecht, Netherlands: Springer.

Bass, J., Contant, T., & Carin, A. (2009). *Activities for teaching science as inquiry* (7th ed.). Boston: Allyn & Bacon.

Estrin, J. (2009). *Closing the innovation gap: Reigniting the spark of creativity in a global economy.* New York: McGraw-Hill.

Hannaford, C. (2005). *Smart moves: Why learning is not all in your head.* Salt Lake City, UT: Great River Books.

Michalewicz, Z., & Michalewicz, M. (2008). *Puzzle-based learning: An introduction to critical thinking, mathematics, and problem solving.* Melbourne, Australia: Hybrid Publishers.

Sutman, F., Schmuckler, J., & Woodfield, J. (2008). *The science quest: Using inquiry/discovery to enhance student learning, grades 7–12.* San Francisco: Jossey-Bass.

Tomlinson, C., Brimijoin, K., & Narvaez, L. (2008). *The differentiated school: Making revolutionary changes in teaching and learning.* Alexandria, VA: Association for Supervision and Curriculum Development.

RESOURCES AND SUGGESTED READINGS

Adams, D., & Hamm, M. (1998). *Collaborative inquiry in science, math, and technology.* Portsmouth, NH: Heinemann.

Armstrong, T. (2000). *Multiple intelligences in the classroom* (2nd ed.). Alexandria, VA: Association for Supervision and Curriculum Development.

Association for Supervision and Curriculum Development (ASCD). (2009). *21st century skills: Promoting creativity and innovation in the classroom.* Alexandria, VA: ASCD.

Benjamin, A. (2003). *Differentiated instruction: A guide for elementary teachers.* Larchmont, NY: Eye on Education.

Browne, M. N., & Keeley, S. M. (2000). *Asking the right questions: A guide to critical thinking* (6th ed.). Upper Saddle River, NJ: Prentice Hall.

Carr, N. (2009). *The big switch: Rewiring the world, from Edison to Google.* New York: W.W. Norton.

City, E. A., Elmore, R. F., Fiarman, S. E., & Teitel, L. (2009). *Instructional rounds in education: A network approach to improving teaching and learning.* Cambridge, MA: Harvard Education Press.

Costantino, P., De Lorenzo, M., & Kobrinski, E. (2006). *Developing a professional teaching portfolio: A guide for success* (2nd ed.). Boston: Allyn & Bacon (Pearson Education).

Drapeau, P. (2004). *Differentiated instruction: Making it work.* New York: Teaching Resources (Scholastic).

Gardner, H. (2006). *Multiple intelligences: New horizons.* New York: Basic Books.

Hassard, J. (1990). *Science experiences: Cooperative learning and the teaching of science.* Menlo Park, CA: Addison-Wesley.

Helprin, M. (2009). *Digital barbarism: A writer's manifesto.* New York: HarperCollins.

Horvitz, E. (2009, July). Minds, machines, and intelligence: A conversation with Eric Horvitz. In Proceedings of *Mainstream of Artificial Intelligence and Intelligence Explosion Risks,* sponsored by the Association for the Advancement of Artificial Intelligence.

Jacobs, H. (Ed.). (2004). *Getting results with curriculum mapping.* Alexandria, VA: Association for Supervision and Curriculum Development.

Marzano, R. J. (2007). *The art and science of teaching: A comprehensive framework for effective instruction.* Alexandria, VA: Association for Supervision and Curriculum Development.

Restak, R. M. (2009). *Think smart: A neuroscientist's prescription for improving your brain's performance.* New York: Riverhead Books.

Starr, L. (2004). Strategy of the week. *Education World.* Available at www.education-world.com/a_curr/strategy/strategy046.shtml (this online site is a place where teachers can share ideas and lesson plans).

Tomlinson, C. (2003). *Fulfilling the promise of the differentiated classroom: Strategies and tools for responsive teaching.* Alexandria, VA: Association for Supervision and Curriculum Development.

Tomlinson, C., & Eidson, C. (2003). *Differentiation in practice: A resource guide for differentiating curriculum, grades 5–9.* Alexandria, VA: Association for Supervision and Curriculum Development.

2

Creative and Innovative Thinking

Differentiated Inquiry, Open-Ended Problem Solving, and Innovation

Imagination is the beginning of creation
You imagine what you desire
You will what you imagine
You create what you will

—George Bernard Shaw[1]

Definitions vary greatly, but academic thinking skills are the mental processes needed to organize, understand, and apply certain principles of complex subjects like math and science. Critical thinking might be thought of as an intellectually disciplined way of actively and skillfully conceptualizing, analyzing, synthesizing, and applying information. Creative and innovative thinking, our primary focus, involves generating original ideas and responses to problems or situations. Creative expression has a lot to do with original insight, self-expression, and communication.

Of course, the different types of thinking skills frequently overlap and reinforce each other. Developing powerful ideas has a lot to do with being able to challenge the conventional approaches we all employ to make sense of our world.

Creative and innovative thinking, along with problem solving and inquiry, are being included among the basic skills needed for the twenty-first century (Copley, 2003). Observation, calculation, experiences, reflection, reasoning, and communication can all serve as a guide to understanding, belief, and action. Standards-based mathematics instruction is built on the belief that teachers must create opportunities for students to make connections between concepts and thoughtfully solve problems through reasoning.

29

When it comes to the scientific inquiry, students are encouraged to ask questions, investigate, and use evidence to come up with imaginative answers. *Problem solving* is at the heart of mathematics; *inquiry* is equally important to science education. Both are compatible with developing highly refined reasoning skills. And both can thrive when differentiated learning is used as an instructional framework for encouraging creativity and innovative ideas in the classroom.

Differentiated instruction (DI) is an approach designed to help teachers figure out *how* to teach, while subject matter standards set out to suggest *what* should be taught. DI involves making subjects more accessible to a wider array of student interests, needs, and learning styles. It recognizes the fact that learners have views, perspectives, preferences, and strengths that need to be taken into account.

When teachers combine opportunities for choice and discovery with intelligent risk taking, the result is often the bubbling up of innovative energy and imaginative ideas. As far as classroom implementation is concerned, if we can imagine it and gather the strength of will to sustain it, then we can create it.

THOUGHTFUL PROBLEM SOLVING AND INQUIRY

Viewing math and science as creative subjects amplifies subject matter competency, thinking skills, and innovative tendencies (Schliemann, Carraher, & Brizuela, 2007). Innovation is where thinking meets up with problems and inquiry to do new things and old things in new ways. Creative and innovative thinking is now such an important part of analytical problem solving in math and collaborative inquiry in science that it can't be ignored. The worth of the ideas created has a lot to do with how the problem being explored is defined.

Later in this chapter, you will find standards-based activities that are designed to help students open new doors to thinking and learning possibilities in math, science, and technology. Along with content, the emphasis is on thinking, not telling students what to think.

In a differentiated classroom, a student's readiness, interests, learning profile, and teamwork skills all matter. Collaborative thoughtfulness goes hand in hand with intellectual curiosity and open-minded persistence. Good teachers know that it is possible to respond to differing needs even when students are working with a partner or in small groups. This is especially true if lessons are designed so that they are meaningful for every individual. Also, the creative and critical imagination is amplified by appealing to different interests in a community of responsible and reflective learners.

Teachers who choose to differentiate lessons begin where students are and build on the belief that students learn in quite different ways. The basic idea is that varying the speed and complexity of instruction helps each individual reason and learn as deeply and as efficiently as possible. To increase student motivation, teachers often encourage students to put thinking skills to work in analyzing and solving problems that are part of the world within which they live. Whether it's in or out of school, innovation does not occur in a vacuum; rather, it draws on the ability to acquire knowledge and apply it in new situations.

Annoying speedbumps are one of the costs of innovation. At any age, innovators must trust themselves to push through roadblocks to achieve their vision; at the same time, they must balance being open to new ideas and continual self and peer assessment. Throughout the process of identifying needs, asking good questions, and trying out new ideas, self-confidence without sufficient questioning is a recipe for disaster.

Nurturing the idea that twenty-first-century innovation involves risk and effort is part of helping students come up with fresh answers to the questions posed and the data collected. Teachers can promote creativity by making collaboration a normal part of the daily routine and encouraging students to express themselves using multiple media.

The fact that the basic skills of one generation may prove inadequate for the next makes it difficult for teachers, parents, communities, and the students themselves. Many factors that influence thinking are generated far from the educational and family world. Popular culture may be an oxymoron, but children who grow up in a nonlinear world of television, computers, video games, and the Internet may have an advantage over adults in adapting to the chaotic world of technological change.

Will the future place a higher value on the length of a person's attention span or on their ability to do many things at the same time? With a multitasking tidal wave crashing over today's youngsters, it seems unlikely they will be as able as their elders when it comes to sustaining the more linear aspects of thoughtful inquiry. However this all gets sorted out, don't be surprised if creativity and innovation become part of the fabric of basic skills needed for the twenty-first century.

As Americans discovered after World War II, big investments in innovation, research, and education (human capital) lead to the dissemination and commercialization of new ideas. Science, technology, and innovation are still keys to the future. Economic growth comes from new techniques and processes, which have no other fuel but imagination.

One of the things that hasn't changed in the twenty-first century is that a nation's growth depends on some combination of natural resources, ideas, and innovation. Those with a lot of financial resources should "take the

money and invest it in innovation, which means education, entrepreneur-
ship, ideas."[2]

THE SOCIETAL IMPACT ON CREATIVE
AND CRITICAL THINKING

Thinking skills, particularly those related to innovation, extend over time
and have a lot to do with originality, adaptiveness, and accomplishment.
New curriculum standards and teaching methods pay closer attention to
problem solving and inquiry related to the world outside of school.

One of the ways of doing this is by encouraging student thought processes
that are similar to those used by mathematicians, scientists, and technology
experts as they go about designing real-world applications. Mathematicians
and scientists collect data, select out information, and reflect on what it
might mean for the natural world.

As students develop similar thinking skills, it becomes more natural to
approach a task in an unconventional, spontaneous, flexible, and original
manner. Sometimes this is done within a preexisting paradigm; sometimes
it means breaking out of conventional boundaries.

Creative and innovative thinking are constructed by the mind and
strongly influenced by personal experience. Various attributes of thoughtfulness (like intelligence, personality, and values) can naturally develop
along with math, science, and technology skills. Science, for example,
teaches respect for evidence, doubt, and opposing points of view. The
quality of an individual's thinking is also influenced by their personal, academic, and cultural backgrounds.

Various elements of thoughtfulness develop along with other attributes
of functional intelligence and personality. Using math, science, and related
technological tools forces us to change ourselves by making us think and
rethink what we know. As students go about this process, they grow better
at reasoning inductively and deductively across the curriculum (Brandt,
2009).

Being good at thinking means being able to form alternative explanations and demonstrate intellectual curiosity in a manner that is flexible,
elaborate, and novel to the thinker. As part of their responsibility to the
future, teachers must respect the unique ideas developed by children and
encourage the development of thinking skills. It seems clear that many
future problems will be solved by people who are flexible, open, original,
and creatively productive.

Good creative and innovative thinking activities encourage students to
analyze underlying assumptions that influence meanings and interpreta-

tions of information. Such intellectually demanding thinking leads children to identify, clarify, problem solve, and become more innovative.

The questions explored can be as general as "Are there limits to how much of the physical universe we can understand?" and "How secure are the foundations of knowledge in science and mathematics?" Questions can be as specific as "How did you figure that one out?" or "What does it mean?" The wording may be changed, but children are never too young to analyze the underlying assumptions that influence meanings. And, they are never too young to question the interpretation of findings and participate in the act of knowledge creation.

There is always the danger of weakening creative and innovative possibilities. We undermine our chances by getting caught up in what David Whyte calls

the eddies and swirls of everyday existence.
I turned my face for a moment and it became my life.[3]

Reasoning, criticism, logical analysis, searching for supporting evidence, and evaluating outcomes might all be considered part of critical thinking. Activities that support this involve clarifying problems, considering alternatives, strategic planning, problem solving, and analyzing the results. Creative thinking may be viewed as fluency, flexibility, originality, and elaboration.

The skills developed in this area would result in the creation of unique expressions, original conceptions, novel approaches, and demonstrations of the ability to see things in imaginative and unusual ways. Problem solving and implementation are part of the fabric of all thinking skills. Here, we are less concerned with definitions than we are with encouraging children to develop skills that lead to high-quality creative and innovative thinking and application.

THINKING ACROSS SUBJECTS AND IN EVERYDAY LIFE

One way to look at modes of thought across disciplines is through *symbolic, imagic,* and *affective* thinking. *Symbolic* includes using words, numbers, and other symbol systems. *Imagic* is visual, spatial, tonal, and kinesthetic. It involves the kind of imagery used by mathematicians and architects; sound relationships explored by musicians; and the movement found in sports and dance. *Affective* thinking works with emotions and feeling to direct inquiry. All three modes of thinking build on reasoning and intuiting to connect the analytic to the intuitive.

As Microsoft founder Bill Gates suggested, "You need to understand things in order to invent things beyond them."[4] The power of inquiry in math, science, and technology lies in its possibility for building on alternative ways of knowing. Along with open-ended problem solving, inquiry also encourages diversity of thought and increases the chances of making creative connections. Creativity might be changing how a particular subject is studied or changing some of the elements of personal life.

An innovative mathematician might change the way mathematics is applied to scientific and technological problems. In our personal lives, for example, this could mean changing day-to-day practices to allow for an hour of exercise to improve the general quality of life. An example that is more relevant to children and young adults at school would be clever hypothesis formation.

Effective instruction in mathematics, science, and technology provokes students to create their own questions and think of innovative applications in the world outside of school. As students become interested in such intellectual invention, it is important that the teacher hold off on their judgments and let the evidence itself be the judge.

Mathematicians, scientists, and technology workers use the tools of science and mathematics to collect, examine, and think about data. Conclusions are formulated and outcomes explained. Like scientists, students can reason, analyze, criticize, and advocate—while avoiding dangerous materials and problems that are developmentally inappropriate.

They can also learn to think spontaneously, flexibly, and originally. An understanding of the physical and biological universe is most solid when it builds on a child's own experiences and discoveries. By modeling thoughtful behavior, teachers can help students become self-confident enough to resolve inconsistencies and uncover truths in mathematics, science, and technology.

Developing methods that extend creative, critical, and innovative thinking across the curriculum strategy should be supported by subject matter standards. Making thinking skills part of math and science instruction involves developing the ability to assess information and make creative and critical judgments.

Some teachers integrate thinking skills into each subject in the curriculum. Others directly teach children thinking skills and strategies. Using metacognitive (thinking about thinking) strategies are a second approach. Another conceptual framework synthesizes all three and adds the heavy use of visual images to soften the boundaries of subject matter and encourage thinking across disciplines. Of course, many teachers pragmatically borrow from all the available possibilities to tailor their own lessons for interdisciplinary inquiry in mathematics, science, and technology.

MULTIPLE THINKING POINTS TO KNOWLEDGE

Recognizing thinking skills as directly involved in successful learning throughout the curriculum doesn't come as a surprise to most teachers.

There is, however, a tendency to think of the scientific method and mathematics problem solving as clear and clean: you formulate hypotheses, organize experiments, collect data, analyze, and interpret the findings.

As scientists, mathematicians, and engineers who are doing original work will tell you, the reality is far less clear-cut and tidy. There are many false starts and detours as they work through alternatives to discover relationships and invent new perspectives. What makes it satisfying for many scientists is the sheer power of searching at the frontiers of knowledge. This passion for inquiry and feeling outward into space for new experiences is just as important for children.

Creative and critical thinkers tend to be reflective, to think problems through, to be flexible in considering original solutions, and to be curious enough to pose and expand new questions. The research evidence suggests that giving students multiple perspectives and entry points into subject matter increases thinking and learning (Costa, 2008). The implication here is that ideas about how students learn a subject need to be pluralized.

Almost any important concept can be approached from multiple directions—emphasizing understanding and making meaningful connections across subjects. This means making available learning possibilities and resources (human and technological) that might appeal to pupils with very different learning styles and cultural backgrounds.

Tomorrow's schools will need to incorporate frameworks for learning that build on the multiple ways of thinking and representing knowledge. By organizing lessons that respect multiple entry points to knowledge, teachers can enhance thoughtfulness and make the school a home for inquiry. If many of today's dreams, possibilities, and admired models are going to be put into widespread practice, then we all must be more courageous in helping move good practice from the margins into the schools, the media, and the home.

A child's thinking ability evolves through a dynamic of personal abilities, social values, academic subjects, and out-of-school experiences. We are all involved, directly or indirectly, in the education of children. Revitalizing the educational process means recognizing the incomplete models of how the world works that children bring to school with them. From birth, children are busy making sense of their environment. They do this by curiously grappling with the confusing, learning ways of understanding, developing schemes for thinking, and finding meaning.

As they enter school, children can sing songs, tell stories, and use their own processes of reasoning and intuiting to understand their surroundings. By the time they reach first grade, they have already developed a rich body of knowledge about the world around them. The best beginning can be extended in school when the teacher cultivates a broad disposition to critical thinking throughout the year. Working with natural rhythms is important, but it takes learning-centered instruction to continue the process of developing mature thinkers.

CONSTRUCTIVISM: JOINING THINKING, CONTENT, AND EXPERIENCE

By viewing individual reality as building on real-life experiences, this book borrows heavily from the constructivists. Briefly, constructivism is a learning theory that suggests knowledge is most effectively acquired by evoking personal meaning in the learner. Although there are differences in terminology, there are many similarities with Piagetian theory.

Math, science, and technology lessons may begin with real materials, invite interactive learning, and allow children to explore the various dimensions of thoughtfulness, subject matter, and real-world applications. The goal is to help children construct a new set of expectations and establish a new state of understanding.

When students make sense of something by connecting to a set of personal everyday experiences, constructivists may call it "viable knowledge." Whether or not they are familiar with the terms being tossed about, good teachers have always connected academic goals to practical problem solving and students' life experiences. Using such a real-world base embeds thinking skills into the curriculum so that students are intensely involved in reasoning, elaboration, hypothesis formation, and problem solving. Such inquiry-based learning can't be isolated within rigid disciplinary boundaries.

Developing mature thinkers who are able to acquire and use knowledge means educating minds rather than training memories. Sometimes the acquisition of enhanced thinking skills can be well structured and planned; at other times, it's a chance encounter formed by a crazy collision of elements. The ability to raise powerful interdisciplinary questions about what's being read, viewed, or heard is a dimension of thinking that makes a powerful contribution to the construction of meaning.

When motivated to reason intelligently, children come up with good decision-making options and elaborations. Out of this come insightful creations that suggest possibilities for action. As all of these elements come together, they form the core of effective thinking and learning.

DIMENSIONS OF THINKING

Complex sequences of thinking are required to explore the physical and biological universe. Really proficient learners almost automatically integrate elements of efficient thinking into their repertoire of techniques for meaning making. Students who know the subject and can reason well are less likely to get caught up in scientific misconceptions.

For those who don't find critical and creative thinking quite so automatic, there is good news. Most of these skills can be developed and amplified by effective instruction. There is strong evidence that many students—especially the youngest and lower achievers—need explicit and sustained instruction to become skilled in thinking and monitoring their own thinking processes (Epstein, 2003).

In addition to teaching about specific thinking skills, students need guidance in how to apply these skills to science/math inquiry. Mental autonomy, creative expression, and critical thinking develop most fully when connected to the child's home and school environment. Good intellectual habits and arousing a passion for math science and technology is the best antidote for the many flavors of pseudoscience.

Content knowledge, critical thinking skills, and a certain clarity of logic have proven to be the best guards against innumeracy and para-science. Thinking processes can help us sort out the real from the unreal. They can also help us as we move toward the acquisition of scientific knowledge.

Key indicators of teaching for thoughtfulness include the following:

1. Students are given sufficient time to think before being required to answer questions.
2. Interaction focuses on sustained examination of a few topics rather than superficial coverage of many.
3. The teacher presses students to clarify or justify their opinions rather than accepting and reinforcing them indiscriminately.
4. Interactions are characterized by substantive coherence and continuity.
5. The teacher models the characteristics of a thoughtful person. This means showing interest in students' ideas and their suggestions for solving problems, modeling problem-solving processes rather than just giving answers, and acknowledging the difficulties involved in gaining a clear understanding of problematic topics.
6. Students generate original and unconventional ideas in the course of the interaction (Ritchhart & Perkins, 2008).

Workshops on critical and scientific thinking often focus on four or five dimensions. Many focus on the positive learning attitudes toward and thinking that leads to the acquisition and integration of knowledge. This way, content is tied to the teaching of thinking.

The basic idea is to work toward developing the thinking involved in refining and extending knowledge, productive habits of the mind, and the thoughtful use of knowledge. Regardless of the approach, the six steps shown above have proven popular with math and science educators. This is partly because they are compatible with content, collaborative interaction, and what teachers are learning about mathematical reasoning, scientific processes, problem solving, and real-world applications.

THE DIMENSIONS OF GOOD THINKING
AND STAFF DEVELOPMENT

Implementing new approaches to learning about mathematics, science, and technology depends on teachers who are open to new ideas and purposely invite reflective thinking. This means that both prospective and practicing teachers need some practical experiences in problem solving and inquiry. Workshops, conferences, and university-level classes can help. This is especially true if they provide a way for teachers to learn how to apply mathematical and science concepts within a context similar to the one they will use with their students.

When carried out over time, professional development activities have proven useful in helping teachers organize instruction to accommodate new ways of representing and imparting knowledge (Rhoton & Bowers, 2001). Clearly, the result of good *pre-* and *in-*service work expands horizons and organizational possibilities.

Critical and creative thinking are natural human processes that can be amplified by awareness and practice. Creative, critical, and innovative thinking makes use of core thinking skills. Classroom instruction and guided practice in the development of these skills will include the following:

1. *Focusing Skills*—attending to selected chunks of information. Some focusing skills include defining, identifying key concepts, recognizing the problem, and setting goals.
2. *Information-Gathering Skills*—becoming aware of the substance or content needed. Observing, obtaining information, forming questions, and clarifying through inquiry are some skills of information gathering.
3. *Remembering Skills*—involving information storage and retrieval. Encoding and recalling are thinking skills that have been found to improve retention. These skills involve strategies such as rehearsal, mnemonics, visualization, and retrieval.
4. *Organizing Skills*—arranging information so it can be understood or presented more effectively. Some of these organizing skills consist of comparing, classifying (categorizing), ordering, and representing information.
5. *Analyzing Skills*—classifying and examining information of components and relationships. Analysis is at the heart of critical thinking. Recognizing and articulating attributes and component parts, focus-

ing on details and structure, identifying relationships and patterns, grasping the main idea, and finding errors are elements of analysis.

6. *Generating Skills*—using prior knowledge to add information beyond what is known or given. Connecting new ideas, inferring, identifying similarities and differences, predicting, and elaborating adds new meaning to information. Generating involves such higher order thinking as making comparisons, constructing metaphors, producing analogies, providing explanations, and forming mental models.

7. *Integrating Skills*—putting things together, solving, understanding, forming principles, and composing and communicating. These thinking strategies involve summarizing, combining information, deleting unnecessary material, graphically organizing, outlining, and restructuring to incorporate new information.

8. *Evaluating Skills*—assessing the reasonableness and quality of ideas. Skills of evaluation include establishing criteria and proving or verifying data (Marzano, Pickering, & Pollock, 2004).

Students have to be able to do more than find information. They also have to be able to evaluate information in a rapidly changing technological environment. Whether it is a website or book, the first step is questioning the source. It is important to build knowledge based on quality information. When using Wikipedia, for example, it is important to know that anyone with access to the Internet can contribute.

Eventually, someone corrects false information, but students need to critically question what they read. Regardless of the source, it is important to *verify* what's found by checking several other sources before seriously considering information.

For teachers to build a solid base of thinking skills into daily math, science, and technology lessons, they must consciously question and reflect on the best approach. Introspective questions about the characteristics of effective instruction help—for example, "How can I get students to focus their thinking, ask questions, retrieve new information, and generate new ideas for analysis?"

To generate ideas, try the following: Think of something and combine it with something else. Adapt whatever you came up with in a way that changes it. Put it to some other use. Eliminate some small part and go on to reverse or rearrange it. What new or innovative ideas emerge?

MULTIPLE WAYS OF THINKING AND APPLYING

Beyond using manipulatives in math and inquiry in science, teachers are bringing these subjects to life by setting thoughtful application problems in real-life contexts. Knowledge is particularly useful when it can be applied or used to create new knowledge. Students need opportunities to use their knowledge to compose, make decisions, solve problems, and conduct research to discover more. As teachers facilitate activities built on multiple ways of reasoning, doors are opened to the physical and biological universe.

The infusion of creative and innovative thinking into the math and science curriculum goes hand in hand with the basic principles students must learn to be competent in these subjects. Solid reasoning supports the foundation of interdisciplinary inquiry, real-world applications, and the production of new knowledge.

In our efforts to bring science and math to life by making it relevant to students' daily lives, it is important to leave spaces where students and teachers can reflect on what they are doing and figure out where they will use the skills they are learning. Creativity and innovation have as much to say to government, business, and education as they do to creative fields like the arts and sciences.

People who think creatively have the ability to produce and consider many alternatives—creating or elaborating on original ideas. Creative and innovative thinkers have the ability to see multiple solutions. Developing and expressing emotional awareness is also a part of creative thinking. This is frequently done by perceiving and creating images that are vivid, strong, and alive from both internal and external vantage points.

Making use of imagination, movement, and sound in playful and useful ways is another element of creative thinking. Overcoming limitations and creating new solutions, using humor, predicting consequences, and planning ahead are other elements. While mathematics and science can lead you toward truth, only imagination can lead you to meaning.

Students will learn elements of creative and innovative thinking from interpersonal communication behaviors. These are developed in a variety of ways: listening, speaking, arguing, problem solving, clarifying, and creating (Dissanayake, 1992). Pairs of students can argue an issue with other pairs and then switch sides.

The chaos and dissonance of group work can help foster thinking and imaginative language development. This way, students learn to work creatively with conflicts, viewing them as possibilities for the improvement of literacy. Hopefully, some of this will carry over to conflict resolution and peer resolution of other disputes.

Thinking does not thrive in a threatening and intimidating environment where either adult or peer pressure impedes independence. Classrooms organized for creative math and science group work can easily learn to function as a community that respects and supports individual learners.

Good teachers support diverse thinking styles and collaboration, helping all students to think and step outside of subject matter and experience boundaries to construct meaning. This means that the teacher and students open themselves up to suggestions, styles of thinking, connections, and ambiguities previously unexamined. The potential for imaginative action grows out of this process. As Aristotle suggested, there are two steps to doing anything: *Make up your mind*, and *Do it!*

ENCOURAGING THE DEVELOPMENT OF THINKING SKILLS

The test of a first-rate intelligence is the ability to hold two opposed ideas in the mind at the same time, and still function.

—F. Scott Fitzgerald[5]

For the twenty-first century, the ability to do a whole host of complicated tasks at the same time (multitasking) may prove crucial. For those who have trouble even walking and chewing gum at the same time, there is trouble ahead. The multidimensional search for meaning is made easier when there is a supportive group climate for generating questions and investigating possibilities.

Critical and creative thinking questions may also come into play after solutions are put forward. Ask students to analyze problems they have solved. As they examine how underlying assumptions influence interpretations, children can be pulled more deeply into a topic. And by evaluating their findings on the basis of logic, there arise other possibilities.

The following encourage the development of thinking skills:

- Provide opportunities for students to explore different viewpoints and domains of information that arouse frustration or outrage.
- Conduct debates and discussions on controversial issues that somehow connect to science, mathematics, and technology. Students work in groups to present an argument on a topic and present their view to another group. Sides can then be switched, the opposite view defended, and different routes to a better social order explored.
- Have students role play historical events or current news happenings from conflicting viewpoints. Examine some of the more questionable television news images or odd points made about current events on a website where the power may be palpable but whose connection to reality is tenuous.
- Encourage students to explore Internet websites that present different viewpoints. For homework, you might have them watch a newscast or

program on TV (e.g., those that interview individuals with differing perspectives on a problem).

- Have students write letters to a newspaper editor, TV producer, congressman, popular journal, or website expressing their stance on an issue of importance.

These suggestions open up the possibility for developing thinking by practicing argumentative thinking skills in small groups. The basic goal is to stimulate and encourage a wide range of collaboration, divergent thinking, and discussion. By arguing important moral dilemmas in science, medicine, technology, politics, literature, art, music, or sports, students can learn content, reason possibilities, and extend ethical concepts.

To have power over the story that dominates one's life in these technologically intensive times means having the power to retell it, deconstruct it, joke about it, and change it as times change. Without this power, it is more difficult to think and act on new thoughts and open the doors to deep thinking.

Beyond specific teaching strategies, the climate of the classroom and the behavior of the teacher are very important. Teachers need to model critical thinking behaviors—setting the tone, atmosphere, and environment for learning.

Being able to collaborate with other teachers can make a formative contribution to how the teacher might better see and construct individual classroom reality. Through collaborative problem solving and inquiry, teachers can help each other in the clarification of goals. They can also share the products of their joint imaginations. Thus, perceptions are changed, ideas flow, and practice can be meaningfully strengthened, deepened, and extended. Like their students, teachers can become active constructors of knowledge.

ENCOURAGING INNOVATIVE THINKING

One Teacher's Checklist

- In what situations did students have to deal with more than one possibility?
- In what ways were students asked to think of new ideas or approaches?
- In what situations were students encouraged to take reasonable risks?
- How were critical and creative thinking skills apparent in the classroom?

- How were multiple intelligences and learning styles considered?
- How often was guessing, hypothesizing, and collaboration encouraged?

The old view of teaching as the transmission of content has been expanded to include new intellectual tools and new ways of helping students thoughtfully construct knowledge on their own and with peers. Teachers who invite thoughtfulness understand that knowledge is to be shared or developed rather than held by the authority. They arrange mathematics instruction so that children construct science/math concepts *and* develop their thinking skills. As a result, everyone involved becomes an active constructor of knowledge and more capable of making thoughtful decisions in the future.

Recognizing the development of thinking skills is a good first step toward its application and assessment. Some possible guideposts for assessing development of self-reliant thinking and collaboration include the following:

- A decrease in "How do I do it?" questions (students asking group members before asking the teacher)
- Using trial and error discovery learning without frustration
- Questioning peers and teachers (asking powerful why questions)
- Using metaphor, simile, and allegory in speaking, writing, and thinking
- Developing interpersonal discussion skills for shared inquiry
- Increasing ability to work collaboratively in cooperative groups
- Increasing willingness to begin a task
- Initiating inquiry
- Increasing comfort with ambiguity and open-ended assignments
- Synthesizing and combining diverse ideas

It's hard to measure attitudes, thinking, and interpersonal skills on a paper and pencil test. Another way is to observe the humor, anecdotes, parental reactions, and teacher-student interactions. The ability of both students and teachers to pull together as a team influences how well students reflect on their thinking, pose powerful questions, and connect diverse ideas. Failure to cultivate these aspects of thinking may be a major source of difficulty when it comes to learning content (Marzano, Pickering, & Pollock, 2004).

POWERFUL IDEAS CAN ILLUMINATE LEARNING

A curriculum that ignores students' powerful ideas will miss many opportunities for illuminating the human condition. To teach content without regard for self-connected thinking prevents subject matter knowledge from being transformed in the student's mind. When it comes to teaching math, science, and technology, lessons that open doors to the unfamiliar and reasoned decision making are just as important as developing specific knowledge and skills. In addition, a curriculum that takes students' thinking seriously is more likely to be successful in cultivating thoughtfulness *and* subject matter competence.

Respecting unique thought patterns and ideas can also be viewed as a commitment to caring communication and openness. Breaking out of established patterns can be done collectively or individually by those most directly involved. All of us need the occasional push or encouragement to get out of our routines.

It's important for teachers to develop their own reflection, problem-solving, and inquiry skills so they can become students of their own thinking. When a teacher decides to participate with students in learning to think on a daily basis, they nourish human possibilities. Can teachers make a difference? Absolutely. The idea is to connect willing teachers with high-quality methods and materials so they can build learning environments that are sensitive to students' growing abilities to think for themselves.

By promoting thoughtful learning across the full spectrum of personalities and ways of knowing, teachers can make a tremendous difference and perform a unique service for the future. When the ideal and the actual are linked, the result can produce a dynamic, productive, and resilient form of learning.

What we know is that teaching and thinking are increasingly being put into practice in a growing number of classrooms and schools (Trefil, 2008). Today's standards-driven programs recognize that powerful problem solving and inquiry can help students make the kind of personal discoveries that change thinking. When math, science, and technology are coupled with the intellectual tools and creative and innovative thinking, unexamined beliefs can be turned into reasoned ones.

THINK-PAIR-SHARE DISCUSSION POINTS FOR TEACHERS

(Some of these points might work equally well for individual students.)

- When you try to explain something to someone else, you clarify your own thinking and learn more yourself.
- It helps the learning process when observations and experiences are integrated into a personal framework (memories, associations, feelings, sounds, rules, etc.). The basic idea is to make sure that an individual

improves her or his ability to explain, predict, provide analogies, make connections, and consider different perspectives.

- By nurturing informed thinking and awareness, teachers help students learn how to actively apply knowledge, solve problems, and enhance conceptual understanding. As children use these processes to change their own theories and beliefs, they grow in ways that are personally meaningful. In developing conceptual understanding by looking at math and science from new angles, students integrate content and thinking skills into their personal experience.

1. Develop Thinking Skills

Students who are exposed to a variety of viewpoints through various media and authentic materials need to be able to view the varying perspectives critically. Active learning, the nurturing of critical thinking skills, rather than passive listening, will enable students to develop self-reliance in their analysis of both literature and the media.

One means of encouraging active learning is to shift the focus from a teacher-centered approach to one that is student centered. Within this framework, the teacher serves as a facilitator of thinking, rather than an authority figure who transmits knowledge. Instead of the traditional lecture/ question approach, students are assigned a specific investigative task that can be accomplished through active teamwork.

2. Shift the Learning Emphasis

In the student-centered class, the emphasis shifts from product to process, from a goal-oriented approach to learning to one in which the learning process is itself the central focus. Less really can be more when it comes to thoughtful connections to science, math, and technology content.

Learning involves not merely the acquisition of information but also the development of critical skills for evaluating facts and the interpretation of facts. Sharing various interpretations of a text adds an extra dimension in the learning process as students not only learn how others perceive a certain issue but also appreciate the various reasoning processes and life experiences that support a different interpretation.

3. Teach Thinking Skills

The thinking skills that can be developed include the following: questioning the presentation of information; the order in which facts are presented; the emphasis of certain facts over others; and the implicit slant of any "story" whether it be in literature, science books, or the mathematically based items (charts, graphs, polls, etc.) in the news. Students can also learn to look for discrepancies between the facts and the conclusions drawn from them or inconsistencies among the various versions of a particular news story.

When reading about scientific discoveries, learners can discuss the varying perspectives among the characters and, for older students, the different points of view between the narrator and the characters. It is important to learn how to distinguish between fact and opinion. Is there any totally objective presentation of information?

4. Analyze Stereotypes

As students learn about the perspectives of other cultures, the varying interpretations of breakthroughs in science, mathematics, and technology should be included. Technological developments in times of war—from the atomic bomb in the United States to V2 rockets in Germany—can be viewed as necessity being the mother of invention.

Students may critically view their own culture's interpretation of such events and explore where stereotypes come from. In this framework, each student's cultural background is viewed as a valuable tool for learning, a bridge to another worldview, rather than as a barrier to understanding another individual.

Understanding the essence of the argument means understanding some of the universal truths that speak to everyone *and* recognizing how a diversity of new voices can add vigor to learning. As students learn about the perspectives of other cultures—including social and historical background—they can explore where stereotypes come from.

This shouldn't stand in the way of supplying students with the common and universal roots of present conditions. It means a more integrative understanding of human community and an appreciation of overlapping cultural experiences. It also means including active learning techniques where students can collaboratively shape alliances that view each student's cultural background as a valuable tool for learning and a vista from which they may see and hear anew.

5. Explore Historical Questions

A middle school example is "How might the Renaissance boom in art and architecture be traced to Italian bankers' application of Eastern and Arabic mathematics to finance?"

Why is the history of science full of innovative ideas that several people had at about the same time?

Have your students find and explore some examples.

6. Use Moral Dilemma (Debate) Activities

Argument (debate) may make some people uncomfortable, but it does result in an understanding of the issues. Bringing important controversial issues out in the open is central to the health and vitality of American education. Encouraging students to argue together can help them reason together (just make sure that each side has an equal chance to be heard). You can get a wide range of interesting responses from questions like the following:

"What does it mean to be human?"
"What might the world be like in twenty-five years?"
"Is the ability to connect with just about anyone at any time worth the invasion of privacy?"

7. Data Collection and the Erosion of Privacy

There is usually no requirement to keep records, but when they are kept they are fair game for lawyers and public viewing. With so much information out there, supply creates demand. It is therefore no wonder that journalists are often advised to destroy their notes every few months. When it comes to viewing a website or buying things in a store, there is money to be made from keeping track of what you're doing. The Electronic Frontier Foundation calls this "the surveillance business model."[6]

What do you think of businesses being able to track just about everything you purchase? What do you think about AT&T promising to route your phone calls and not let anyone listen in . . . and then cooperating with the government's surveillance of telephone calls and Internet communications? (By the way, some telecommunication companies refused to go along with the request to collect information; others said they would only do it with a warrant.)

ACTIVITIES FOR STUDENTS

"Writing" a Photo Essay on the World of Work

Original photo essays can be done in the community or at school. They involve predicting, observing, analyzing functional relationships, taking pictures, interviewing, and viewing how a variety of occupations apply strategies to solve problems on the job. This activity will help students connect to the world of future work possibilities and understand their relationship to the adult world.

If the school is used, students should include everyone who comes into the school—from firefighters to university supervisors looking in on student teachers. Students might examine magazines, newspapers, the Internet, and company brochures to see how some stories emphasize pictures.

1. Before observing or asking how a person in a particular occupation works, make a list of what you think the person does. Write a paragraph summarizing your predictions.
2. Check on the accuracy of your predictions and write a paragraph after observing or having a discussion with the subject. Decide how you may have been wrong early on, and add new information after observation and/or discussion.

If you can observe the person at work, take ten pictures of your subject doing different things. Use captions to explain what's going on. Emphasize pictures of problems the person has to understand and plans he or she has to devise, carry out, and evaluate. Keeping in mind the results of the first two sections, prepare a set of five general questions to ask the subject, for example, "What do you do at school, and what training did you do to get the job?" Next, ask five specific questions based on what you noticed when you were observing the subject.

A flaw of any kind can create mystery—and mystery leads to a heightened desire to understand.

To structure the *Photo Essay*, proceed as follows: First, provide a brief introduction to get your "reader" interested. Next, use six or seven of your favorite pictures and list the topic and a caption by each photograph. End the work with a paragraph or two summing up the pictures and leaving readers with what you want them to think about. The end result can be photocopied larger, laminated, provided with graphs, and put up in the classroom or around the school.

CLEARING THOUGHTFUL PATHWAYS TO MATH AND SCIENCE

As far as math and science are concerned, broad misconceptions, naive theories, oversimplified explanations, and stereotyping often rule the day. Just ask students to draw a picture of a mathematician or scientist, and see what they come up with. Start by having individual students create their own drawing, then share with a partner or small group. The final step is having each group present an example to the whole class for discussion.

Be sure they discuss the difference between drawings and reality. Bringing stereotypes or misconceptions to the surface is not all that difficult, but intelligently dealing with the results requires an in-depth and thoughtful awareness of the subject matter.

Clearing up misunderstandings and exploring subject matter realities are more meaningful when students are connected by a variety of paths to real situations. In fact, few concepts are too difficult when the ideas at the heart of a subject have meaning for students' lives. In a search for meaning, teachers and peers can help individuals understand the personally connected nature of a subject—while leaving room to reshape concepts as new information becomes available.

The personal search for understanding thinking (metacognitive awareness) is shaped by the students' attitudes, the subject matter, knowledge of themselves, and their ability to work with others. Topics can be explored using different methods: descriptive accounts, logical/analytical/quantitative methods, and aesthetic expressions in art, dance, or music.

Lessons can be a pattern similar to the following:

- forming a topic
- exploring prior knowledge
- sharing interesting new questions
- researching a specific knowledge base
- comparing, reporting, and thinking reflectively about a project
- expressing the positive and negative conclusions to an audience

For teachers, it's a question of figuring out how to divide their efforts so they can instruct students with different backgrounds, needs, skill levels, and interests.

INVITING THOUGHTFULNESS AND EXTENDING KNOWLEDGE

Mathematicians and scientists set out to do some combination of *discovering* and *constructing* the truth. Many disciplines may *interpret*, but math and science help *reveal* the realities of the natural world as they exist in an empirical universe. It was Galileo, by the way, who said that math was the natural language of the universe.

We are far from having all the answers needed to design a curriculum that invites students into a full and thoughtful understanding of mathematical problem solving, inquiry, and the scientific method (processes). But we do know enough to begin the intellectual adventure. And, we know enough to institute educational practices that promote true understanding. Reflecting, discussing, and cultivating the disposition for thoughtfulness can inform and enrich our teaching. Whether it's the teacher or a student, asking *why* always helps. The same can be said for developing a sense for asking the right questions—and being able to seek the right answer.

A skilled teacher, open to new ideas, can open a number of doors to adventures in imaginativeness and creative perception. The goal is to integrate, extend, refine, and use knowledge meaningfully. This requires skilled teachers to integrate and fit what is known about promoting creativity and innovation into the instructional process. Educators also need all the help they can get as they work to create vital learning communities that foster critical, creative, civic, and moral thought.

Although improvements in teaching alone will not solve some of our most dire social and educational problems, teachers have an absolutely vital role to play in student success. Also, teachers who have a substantial knowledge of pedagogy and subject matter can use their classroom expertise in a manner that gradually legitimizes new approaches. What challenges might your students be facing in the next fifteen or twenty years?

No one can play it safe and easy when it comes to breaking down the barriers between social problems and educational opportunities. The same can be said for mathematical problem solving and scientific inquiry. Courage and support are needed for individuals to take intelligent risks. Both teachers and students should know that, when it comes to innovation, some things work and some things don't. What's important is learning from mistakes. Making mistakes has to be viewed as part of being good at any job. There is, after all, no one in the universe who can fail exactly like you can. So, don't waste too much time worrying about it.

Like mathematicians and scientists, teachers can only bring about real change in their field by having the courage, freedom, and support to succeed by sometimes failing. It's much like innovation: some things do work—and some things don't. But if you don't try, enthusiasm can go stale in a hurry.

If given the chance, good teachers, with good approaches, can push the process of more effective thinking and learning forward. Clearly, they can make a real difference in helping students learn math, science, technology, and just about everything else.

> Good teachers put snags in the river of children passing by, and over the years, they redirect hundreds of lives. Many people find it easy to imagine unseen webs of malevolent conspiracy in the world, and they are not always wrong. But there is also an innocence that conspires to hold humanity together, and it is made of people who can never know the good that they have done.
>
> —Tracy Kidder[7]

VALUING THOUGHTFULNESS

Subject matter understanding and thinking are not antithetical. Higher-level thinking requires at least some level of content information to be effective.

But no textbook, or even the glut of data on the Internet, is a substitute for thinking. So, it's important to take the time needed to make sure student thinking reaches a level where it can transform content knowledge in a way that makes it transferable to the outside world.

Thinking skills are learned through interaction with the school curriculum, environment, peers, and the mass media. Innovative thinkers seek better ways of doing things. They believe in the power of their mind. Some students pick it up naturally, while others learn reasoning skills with difficulty or not at all.

It is clear that some thinking skills can be taught directly—for example, *generating multiple ideas about a topic, summarizing, figuring out meaning from context, understanding analogy,* and *detecting reasoning fallacies.* Even the length of time a teachers waits ("wait time") after asking a question can make a difference in the quality of a student's thinking. There are times when a three- to five-second pause can add flexibility and creativity to the response (Cole, 2008).

There will *never* be enough time to teach *all* the information we feel is useful. But when there is time for problem solving, inquiry, and reflection, covering less can actually help students learn more deeply. Too much of the math and science curriculum is a little like the Great Salt Lake: roughly twenty miles wide, sixty miles long, and fourteen feet deep. (The size and depth fluctuate substantially due to the shallowness.)

Since it is so difficult to figure out what information will be crucial to students in the future, it makes sense to pay more attention to the *intellectual tools* that will be required in any future. This suggests focusing on how models of critical thought, problem solving, and inquiry can be used differently, at different times, and in different situations.

The idea is to put more emphasis on concepts with high generalizability—like teamwork, reflection, perceptive thinking, self-direction, and the motivation needed for lifelong learning. Learning how to learn is important. It's not always what you know but rather how quickly you can learn it.

Although math, science, and technology are getting more attention than ever, it is important to remind ourselves of the importance of creative and innovative thinking in their own right and in the contributions they can make across the curriculum. For students to learn how to think new thoughts requires teachers who recognize children's need to learn in meaning-centered explorations.

Serendipity often plays a role in developing creative outcomes, so space is needed for making unexpected discoveries when looking for something else. Feeling and meaning can be turned inside out as children and young adults learn how to construct their own knowledge and absorb new experiences in ways that make sense *to them*. Promoting creativity and innovation in the classroom requires going beyond giving students the *truth* of others, making it possible for them to discover their own. This somewhat differentiated approach requires teachers to begin instruction where individual students *are* rather than using a uniform model of pre-scribed lessons.

We know that students learn in a variety of ways and can be encouraged to reach desired goals by very different paths. Children can demonstrate what they have learned about math, science, and technology in a number of ways: videos, performances, photo collages, stories for the newspaper, blogs on the Internet, or other projects that can be shared with other students and members of the community.

This process gets at the essence of what curriculum is: ways of engaging students in thought on matters that are believed to be important—and sharing what they find. To be educated means knowing the depths that wait for us under the surface of things, regardless of what those things may be.

Thinking and its expression in mathematics and science can take many forms. Painting, music, and dance (movement) can resonate with meaning and are just one set of neglected imaginative abilities that can be brought to the fore. The idea is to have students work with various media and sub-ject areas so they can go beyond the literal and linear to probe areas that are ambiguous in meaning and rich in illusion. Creative expression is not limited to writing, drawing, or electronic imagery. As Isadora Duncan made clear, "If I could say it, I wouldn't have to dance it."[8]

When the literary converges with the scientific, it is possible to see the uni-versal residing in the particular. Poetry is a powerful way of doing this—while helping you look out over the horizon. "The Summer Day," a poem by Mary Oliver (1992), says as much about imagining the future as it does about the power of observation and the importance of reflecting on the beauty in the natural world. It can be easily accessed on the Internet—just type "Mary Oli-ver" and "The Summer Day" in a Google search box and you will get multiple possibilities to click on for the full poem. Among other things, she seems to be asking if there is a better way of spending a day (or more) than in observ-ing, appreciating, and understanding the natural world.

Reflection is one of the keys to higher levels of creative and innovative thinking. It requires a combination of time, silence, and discussion for true appreciation and experience. If you allow yourself to get too hurried, you will lose the ability to pay real attention to the world. The glut of information and increased personal connectivity in today's world can overwhelm chil-dren and young adults. This makes taking time for thoughtful reflection— or simply sitting down and reading a book—more difficult than ever.

Innovation involves more than looking at new things in new ways (Von Hippel, 2005). A source of contemplation for the future can be found in collecting, selecting, and contemplating experiences in the present. Some-times, you can do a better job of figuring out what is going to happen in the future by taking the time to imaginatively look around now, rather than just looking ahead.

> The real voyage of discovery consists not in seeking new landscapes, but in having new eyes.
>
> —Marcel Proust[9]

BUILDING DIVERSE BRIDGES
TO AN AMBIGUOUS FUTURE

> Don't tell people how to do things, tell them what to do and let them surprise you with their results.
>
> —George Patton[10]

Learning how to think sometimes means cognitive self-observation and taking part in problem solving and inquiry-rich classroom interaction. Being good at creative and innovative thinking means being able to reason and solve new problems. It doesn't mean repeating memorized words or concepts.

A better approach is engaging in thoughtful instruction that is targeted to the varying learning needs of diverse students. Along the meaning-making way, providing new information and experiences in math or science-centered subjects can help students adapt and evolve mentally (Kuhn, 2008). Students now have to go beyond knowing to understanding how to actually do something with what they know.

Drawing on past experiences and applying them in innovative ways requires that students practice doing so frequently. Expressing, refining, and extending student's reasoning and problem-solving abilities requires that teachers and instructional programs take these skills seriously. When it comes to creative and innovative thinking, teachers can help by modeling the process, stressing firsthand experiences, and arranging class schedules so there is time for immersion in the more imaginative aspects of mathematics, science, and technology.

The implications of pedagogy extend well beyond the classroom. Educators are at the center of the vision of regaining national momentum; this includes adapting to new realities and inculcating numeracy and scientific literacy at all levels of society.

Continuously reevaluating current knowledge is one of the keys to innovative behavior. Moving students from the conventional to the innovative requires the involvement of informed teachers who can make good use of new approaches and prepare students for unexpected challenges and possibilities. When it comes to individual classrooms, informal belief systems are just as important as methodology.

As teachers become students of their own learning, they discover the inconsistencies between what they *believe* about teaching and how they *practice* the art and science of effective instruction. Such thoughtful reflection about practice can play a major role in helping teachers become autonomous professionals. Discoveries that any of us make ourselves are more convincing. By turning on a spotlight that illuminates how well we are helping students understand something, we can make more accurate decisions about instruction and professional development.

Innovative inquiry is not all student generated. Although open-ended problem solving is the opposite of transmitting information, there will always be a place for short lectures and whole-class instruction. By encouraging learners to work with topics and questions, teachers initiate a good way to arouse innovative curiosity, wonder, and the will to pursue questions that have multiple answers—for example, is the Internet becoming a darker cyberspace that reflects the chaos and bad behavior of today's world—or is it becoming more of a place for learning and healthy adventure? If a new Internet was built from scratch, how might security be improved, and how might it be designed to correct some things that the current Internet does poorly, like supporting mobile users?

As science and its associates (math and technology) play a major role in transforming our world, a more educated public is absolutely essential for dealing with a constantly evolving set of aesthetic, moral, political, and economic issues. A good example of what happens when rationality and numeracy (mathematical literacy) are missing from the conversation is the financial crisis that started in 2008.

There were at least a few economists on the sidelines, like Nouriel Roubini, who saw it coming well in advance. But Wall Street and cheerleading financial journalists on TV totally missed the fact that their tidy ecosystem of cause and effect was a house of cards. Although there were exceptions, like *Black Swan* author Nassim Taleb, most of the public went along with the fantasy and never looked at the numbers behind a complex system of assumptions. Even after things clearly started to go bad, *the band played on;* the operative slogan was "the fundamentals of the economy are strong." It wasn't until 2009 that the party was really over.

Don't think that a thoughtful fifth grader can't figure some of this out. As one eleven–year-old said after looking at a graph in the newspaper that showed the collapse of the housing market, "Don't loan money to people who can't pay you back."

Math and science are disciplines that derive information from specific thought processes: observations, establishing the facts, and proposing rational solutions to problems. After working with peers and hypothesizing from what is known, it may be a good idea to test or confirm the hypothesis. In the past, teachers emphasized the rules of mathematics and science. Now, many are making sure that students pay close attention to mathematical problem solving and using scientific methods (processes) of reasoning.

Becoming aware of the outmoded abstractions on which thinking is too often based has a lot to do with mathematical reasoning and scientific inquiry. As Alfred North Whitehead has suggested, "A civilization which cannot burst through its current abstractions is doomed to sterility after a very limited burst of progress."[11] To help students find their way, teachers need to stay current, consider diverse points of few, and look around the corner whenever they can.

SUMMARY AND CONCLUSION

Teachers are responsible for creating a learning environment that ensures the maximum growth of every student. When it comes to math, science, and technology lessons, it helps to differentiate by attending to student differences, thinking skills, and innovative possibilities. But dealing with today's rapidly changing realities is a shared responsibility.

The American K–12 educational system has been neglected at the very time the need for informed public engagement is growing. Public responsibility and participation are, after all, just as important as making sure teachers are familiar with the characteristics of effective instruction and the subjects they teach.

A broadly informed citizenry is the key to strengthening our national capacity for innovation in an increasingly competitive world. This means we have to educate *everyone* to think critically, creatively, and deeply. It also means listening closely to people outside of the usual circle of experts (who usually think they are right) because frequently ignored outliers are more likely to make you look at things in different ways. To solve today's problems—especially if a new approach is needed—you need to do more than round up the usual suspects; other voices must be brought in.

Dealing with complex issues, ambiguity, and change may prove to be essential skills because the circumstances of human existence will experience many startling upheavals during the lifespan of today's elementary and middle school students. Mathematics, science, and technology will surely be at the center of those dramatic changes.

The successful teaching of these subjects depends on teachers who have the vision, intellect, and ability to create lessons that include dynamic inquiry and thoughtful problem-solving experiences. Hopefully, the result will be students who can face problems in a new context, self-correct their own thinking, and adapt in innovative ways.

Today's students have to be prepared to thoughtfully use every tool available to solve problems that are around now. But they also have to be equally prepared to use methods and technologies that have yet to arrive on the scene to solve problems that have yet to be recognized. An education that ignores these new realities is incomplete. And you can be sure that, if we ignore the realm of the imagination and its potential impact on the future, we do so at our own peril.

REFERENCES

Brandt, D. (2009). *Literacy and learning*. San Francisco: Jossey-Bass.

Cole, A. (2008). *Better answers* (2nd ed.). Portland, ME: Stenhouse Publishers.

Copley, A. (2003). *Creativity in education and learning: A guide for teachers and educators*. London: Kogan Page.

Costa, A. (2008). The thought-filled curriculum. *Educational Leadership, 65* (5), 20–24.

Dissanayake, E. (1992). *Homo aestheticus*. New York: Free Press.

Epstein, A. S. (2003). How planning and reflection develop young children's thinking skills. *Young Children, 58* (5), 28–36.

Kuhn, D. (2008). *Education for thinking*. Cambridge, MA: Harvard University Press.

Marzano, R. J., Pickering, D. J., & Pollock, J. E. (2004). *Classroom instruction that works: Research-based strategies for increasing student achievement*. Upper Saddle River, NJ: Prentice Hall.

Rhoton, J., & Bowers, P. (Eds.). (2001). *Professional development: Planning and design*. Arlington, VA: NSTA Press.

Ritchhart, R., & Perkins, D. (2008). Making thinking visible. *Educational Leadership, 65* (5), 57–61.

Schliemann, A., Carraher, D., & Brizuela, B. (2007). *Bringing out the algebraic character of arithmetic: From children's ideas to classroom practice*. Mahwah, NJ: Lawrence Erlbaum.

Trefil, J. (2008). *Why science?* New York: Teachers College Press.

Von Hippel, E. (2005). *Democratizing innovation*. Boston: MIT Press.

Zakaria, F. (2008). *The post-American world*. New York: W.W. Norton.

RESOURCES AND SUGGESTED READINGS

Adams, D., & Hamm, M. (1995). *New designs for teaching and learning: Promoting active learning in tomorrow's schools*. San Francisco: Jossey-Bass.

Atwood, M. (1988). *Cat's eye*. New York: Doubleday.

Baron, J. (1988). *Thinking and deciding*. New York: Cambridge University Press.

Harlen, W. (2009). *The teaching of science in the primary schools*. New York: Routledge.

Hooks, B. (2009). *Teaching critical thinking.* New York: Routledge.

Kidder, T. (1989). *Among schoolchildren.* New York: Houghton Mifflin.

Oliver, M. (1992). A summer day. In *House of light: New and selected poems.* Boston: Beacon Press.

Sternberg, R. (2007). *Wisdom, intelligence and creativity synthesized.* New York: Cambridge University Press.

3

Problem Solving in Mathematics

Creativity and Innovation in a New Age of Numbers

> The world is moving into a new age of numbers. Partnerships between mathematicians and computer scientists are bulling into whole new domains . . .
>
> —Stephen Baker[1]

Math skills are becoming more and more of a practical necessity in a global information-based society. To make math meaningful for all students requires making it developmentally appropriate, working with questions, allowing for depth, and offering challenging activities. When creativity and innovation are added to the equation, it helps if you take the social nature of learning into account.

Mathematical problem solving that involves group interaction and interdependence has been shown to be an effective way to engage students in real-world tasks and experiences. As Lev Vygosky pointed out, *what children can do together today they can do alone tomorrow* (Dixon-Krauss, 1996).

Innovative mathematical problem solving often requires *questioning* and *inquiry*; the result can ignite interest in learning about math. The basic idea is to get students beyond being compliant learners who simply answer questions the teacher asks. When exploring an issue, compliant learners often look for the easy answer, whereas active and thoughtful learners are more likely to search for additional information about the topic. As learners become more creative and innovative, they are also more likely to raise additional questions, inquire more deeply, and offer diverse points of view (Craft, 2005).

Children are born with creative ability, but they need a creativity-friendly math learning environment to develop their full potential. To move beyond someone else's words, ideas, and solutions, students need opportunities to struggle with math-related problems that really interest and motivate them.

Quite simply, problem solving in mathematics is applied thinking. Formulating, defining, implementing, and considering a range of solutions are all part of today's math instruction. Success requires a positive attitude, cognitive skills, open possibilities, and a certain level of mathematical knowledge.

The most dynamic problems are often ill defined and open to a wide range of possible solutions. Creativity and innovation can help because they have a lot to do with adjusting the mind to a diversity of new ideas and unique possibilities. Creative outcomes can be judged on the basis of flexibility, originality, fluency, and elaboration. Organizing at least some of the classwork around essential problems, questions, themes, and big ideas can amplify both thinking skills and content learning.

Math content is one thing; thinking skills and approaches to teaching are quite another. With their classrooms filled with a diverse group of students (who have varying abilities and learning styles), what can teachers do to help each and every student in their classroom succeed? Differentiated instruction (DI) can be a part of the answer; it is a proven approach for teachers who are designing math instruction for students with diverse interests, needs, and ability levels.

MOVING BEYOND STANDARDIZATION
AND COMPUTATION

Standards are one thing, standardization quite another. Traditionally, math lessons were a chalk-and-talk type of whole-group instruction. They usually focused on the computational skills of arithmetic: addition, subtraction, multiplication, and division—along with whole numbers, fractions, decimals, and percentages. The basic arithmetic skills still matter, but today there is general agreement that a deep understanding of mathematics is much more than facts, figures, and computation (NCTM, 2000).

The math standards document from the National Council of Teachers of Mathematics (NCTM) emphasizes teaching mathematical reasoning and problem-solving skills. It is hoped that along the sense-making way, students will develop a positive and confident attitude toward mathematics. Within this context, creative and innovative skills are quite compatible fellow travelers.

Learning for understanding is an important part of today's math instruction; it is a good framework for knowledge application as students learn new concepts and figure out how to solve new problems. In the differentiated classroom, lessons are frequently designed so that students do not have to reach the same goal at the same time. Sometimes, students work alone, but often they work in groups of three or four or in pairs. Learners may solve the same or similar problems, but the individual, group, or think-pair-share strategies used to solve them represent different levels of conceptual understanding.

Typically, students bring varying backgrounds to their math lessons, and teachers have to work hard to accommodate this diversity. On one level, we believe that all students have the potential to learn mathematics. On another level, we have to agree that at least some of our students arrive so unprepared that they encounter academic difficulties.

A major challenge is making sure that even reluctant learners participate in constructing mathematical knowledge. Everyone from math educators to parents and textbook publishers has been working hard to develop effective ways to meet the mathematical learning needs of *all* the students who show up at school.

Students with attention deficit, memory problems, motor disabilities, and visual and auditory difficulties may all require special accommodations during math instruction to reach their potential (White, 2004). With some students, it's not a question of disability or language proficiency; it's a question of motivation and attitude.

But regardless of the source of difficulty, providing reluctant math learners with a strong mathematics program is easier for everybody if teachers differentiate instruction, modify lessons, build teamwork skills, and tap into the natural strength of each student (Benjamin, 2003). As with more successful students, it is best to make sure that reluctant learners understand what it means to *know* and *do* mathematics in and out of school.

DEVELOPING A PERSONAL DEFINITION OF MATHEMATICS AND RELEVANT STUDENT ACTIVITIES

A teacher's view of mathematics will influence how they approach teaching that subject. We all have different ideas about what mathematics is. Which of the following points about mathematics is closest to yours?

1. Mathematics Is a Way of Thinking and Asking Questions

How students make math-related plans, organize their thoughts, analyze data, and solve problems is *doing* mathematics. People comfortable with math are often comfortable with thinking. *The question* is the cornerstone of all investigation. It guides the learner to a variety of sources revealing previously undetected patterns. These undiscovered openings can become sources of new questions that can deepen and enhance learning and inquiry.

Math Activity

List all the situations outside of school in which your group used math during the past week.

2. Mathematics Is an Understanding of Patterns and Relationships

Students need to recognize the repetition of math concepts and make connections with ideas they know. These relationships help unify the math curriculum as each new concept is interwoven with former ideas. Students quickly see how a new concept is similar or different from others they already know. For example, students soon learn how the basic facts of addition and subtraction are interrelated (4 + 2 = 6 and 6 - 2 = 4). They use their observation skills to describe, classify, compare, measure, and solve problems.

A Primary Grade Math Activity

Encourage first- or second-grade math groups to show how one math combination (like 4 + 2 = 6) is related to another basic fact (like 6 - 4 = 2). In later grades, students learn how the basic facts of multiplication and division are interrelated (4 × 3 = 12 and 12 ÷ 3 = 4). They use their observation skills to describe, classify, compare, measure, and solve problems.

3. Mathematics as a Tool

It is what mathematicians use in their work. It is also used by all of us every day. Students come to understand why they are learning the basic math principles and ideas that the school curriculum involves. Like mathematicians and scientists, they also will use mathematics tools to solve problems. They soon learn that many careers and occupations require the use of the tools of mathematics.

Math Activity

Solve this problem using the tools of mathematics: A man bought a junk car for $50 and sold it for $60. Then he bought the car back for $70 and sold it again for $80. How much money did he make or lose? Do the problem with your group and explain your reasoning.

4. Mathematics Is Fun (a Puzzle)

Anyone that has ever worked on a puzzle or stimulating problem knows what we're talking about when we say mathematics is fun. The stimulating quest for an answer encourages learners to find a solution. Innovation fits easily into this process.

Math Activity

With a partner, play a game of cribbage (a card game in which the object is to form combinations for points). Dominoes is another innovative challenging game to play in groups.

5. Mathematics Is an Art

Mathematics is defined by harmony and internal order. Mathematics needs to be appreciated as an art form where everything is related and interconnected. Art is often thought to be subjective, and by contrast objective mathematics is often associated with memorized facts and skills. Yet, the two are closely related to each other. Because teachers tend to focus on the skills, they may forget that students need to be guided to recognize and appreciate the fundamental organization and consistency as they construct their own understanding of mathematics.

Math Activity

Have a small group of students find geographic shapes, label them, and design a picture with them.

6. Mathematics Is a Language, a Means of Communicating

It requires being able to use special terms and symbols to represent information. This unique language enhances our ability to communicate across the disciplines of science, technology, statistics, and other subjects. For example, a struggling learner encountering 3 + 2 = 5 needs to have the language translated to terms he or she can understand. Language is a window into students' thinking and understanding.

Our job as teachers is to make sure students have carefully defined terms and meaningful symbols. Statisticians may use mathematical symbols that seem foreign to some of us, but after taking a statistics class, we too can decipher the mathematical language. It's no different for children. Symbolism, along with visual aids such as charts and graphs, is an effective way of expressing math ideas to others. Students learn to not only interpret the language of mathematics but also *use* that knowledge.

Math Activity

Get into small groups of four or five. Have your group brainstorm about what they would like to find out from other class members (favorite hobbies, TV programs, kinds of pets, etc.). Once a topic is agreed on, have them organize and take a survey of all class members. When the data are gathered and compiled, have groups make a clear, descriptive graph showing the results of the survey; this can be posted in the classroom.

7. Mathematics Is Interdisciplinary

Math works with the big ideas that connect subjects. Mathematics relates to many subjects. Science and technology are the obvious choices. Literature, music, art, social studies, physical education, and just about everything else make use of mathematics in some way.

Math Activity

With a group, design a song using a rhythmic format that can be sung, chanted, or rapped. The lyrics can be written and musical notation added.

You may well pick ideas from several of the above points to explain what you think mathematics is. Have a think-pair-share conversation about your point of view with another teacher.

COLLABORATIVE INQUIRY IN MATHEMATICS

Collaborative inquiry is a way of teaching that builds on group interaction and students' natural curiosity. Teamwork activities can involve pairs of students or small groups. Collaboration works particularly well with problem-solving and inquiry activities where students are striving to develop knowledge and understanding of mathematical ideas.

Through discussion, students can become better at reflection, critical reasoning, and creative thinking. This active process is a powerful vehicle for encouraging students to ask questions, gather data, observe, analyze, propose answers, explain, predict, and communicate the results (Stephen, Bowers, Cobb, & Gravemeijer, 2004).

Collaborative inquiry is supported when students have opportunities to describe their own ideas and hear others explain their thoughts, raise questions, and explore various team approaches. Within a small group setting, students have more opportunities to interact with math content than they do during whole-class discussions.

The role of the teacher is to help students become aware of how to ask questions and how to find evidence. As teachers move away from a "telling" model to "structured group experiences," they encourage students to interact with each other and value social relationships as they become informed investigators.

The challenge for the teacher is to set up group work that engages students in meaningful math activities. Critical thinking occurs when students are encouraged to intelligently challenge the ideas of others.

Discussions and questions help students pay attention to conceptual patterns and universal connections. All students need to be challenged to think and work together to solve problems. The next step is helping them feel secure as they go about debating and imaginatively applying their understandings.

We want all students to be involved in high-quality, engaging mathematics instruction. High expectations should be set for all, with accommodations for those who need them. Students will confidently engage in mathematics tasks, explore evidence, and provide reasoning and proof to support their work. As active resourceful problem solvers, students will be flexible as they work in groups with access to technology. Students value mathematics when they work productively and reflectively as they communicate their ideas orally and in writing (NCTM, 2000).

This is just part of the vision set forth in the NCTM Standards 2000 document. Here we set out to help teachers gain a better understanding of the mathematics standards. Along the way, suggestions are made for blending creative and innovative skills into effective mathematics teaching.

AN OVERVIEW OF THE NCTM STANDARDS FOR SCHOOL MATHEMATICS

The standards are descriptors of the mathematical content and processes that students should learn. They call for a broader scope of mathematics studies, pointing out what should be valued in mathematics instruction. The standards describe a comprehensive foundation of what students should know and be able to do. They state the understandings, knowledge, and skills appropriate for students at different grade levels. Problem solving and inquiry are central concerns.

> The first key to wisdom is constant questioning. . . . By doubting we are led to inquiry, and by inquiry we arrive at the truth.
>
> —Peter Abelard (1125)[2]

We sometimes hear complaints from teachers that local, state, and national standards are telling them how to teach. There is no question that, at some level, content standards often identify *what* you should be teaching. But the standards rarely tell you, for example, *how* to go about teaching mathematics.

Individual teachers usually have a lot of latitude in how they go about teaching content in a way that plays to their strengths as a teacher. For example, if hands-on movement activities are their specialty, it makes sense to take that approach in designing lesson plans. The basic philosophy is don't tell people how to do things; tell them what to do, and let them surprise you with their ingenuity.

Whichever approach the teacher decides to take, one size rarely fits all, and every student should be provided with the opportunity to learn significant mathematics. The *Principles and Standards for School Mathematics* strengthen teachers' abilities to differentiate by including information about the way students develop mathematical knowledge. The standards dealt with here include mathematical content (addressing what students should learn) and process (addressing various aspects of doing mathematics). The content standards point to number, operations, and measurement in describing the foundations of what students should know.

As far as the process is concerned, the math standards suggest problem solving, inquiry, and reasoning. In addition, proof, communicating, making connections, and representing data are considered good ways of expressing, using, and applying mathematical knowledge. The goals articulated by the standards are also responsive to the accelerated changes in our society, schools, and classrooms. Individual teachers can differentiate assignments and make other alterations for students within their classrooms, but it is best if the school itself has a coherent program of mathematics study (Adams, 2000).

It is time to make sure that all Americans are provided with a complete and competitive education. No curriculum should be carved in stone at any level; rather, it must be responsive to the lessons of the past, the concerns of the present, and the innovative human and technological possibilities of the future.

In a world filled with the technological products of math and science, knowing about these subjects is more important than ever. Still, while there has been a lot of attention given to making digital resources available to schools, there hasn't been enough concern about how technology can be employed in creative, innovative, and academically useful ways.

CONNECTING WITH THE MATH CURRICULUM STANDARDS

The next section connects some of the standards to classroom practice by presenting a few sample activities for each standard. The intent is not to prescribe an activity for a unique grade level but rather to present activities that can be used in many grades. Even at a specific grade level, differentiation involves gearing a lesson up for some and down for others.

NUMBER AND NUMBER OPERATIONS STANDARD

I know that two and two make four and should be glad to prove it if I could—although I must say if by any process I could convert 2 & 2 into five it would give me much greater pleasure.

—George Gordon Byron (1812)[3]

Like many innovative thoughts, this one never quite worked out. Later, Lady Caroline Lamb claimed that romantic poet Lord Byron was "mad, bad and dangerous to know."[4] Still, in the twenty-first century there may be a mathematician somewhere who can convert "2 and 2" into five. But don't count on it.

As a branch of mathematics, arithmetic matters; it is the art of making and interpreting numerical models (signs) of commonsense counting notions. Addition, subtraction, multiplication, and division are good examples of the computation or calculation possibilities of arithmetic. As a practical matter, arithmetic and math usually go hand in hand.

Mathematics is the science of numbers and their operations, interrelations, combinations, abstractions, and space configurations. The study of abstract structure is central to math. Also, structure, measurement, estimation, generalizations, and probability play a role in math-based inquiry.

Mathematics has always been some combination of *problem-solving craft* and *theoretical discipline*. Although only a few may become mathematicians, all students need to reach a basic level of competency in concepts and skills related to numbers. All students should be able to represent, analyze, and generalize a variety of patterns with words, graphs, pictures, tables, and charts in a way that helps them explain and solve problems.

Teachers can help learners strengthen their sense of numbers, moving from initial basic counting techniques to a more sophisticated understanding. The goal is to make sense of the ways numbers are used in their everyday world. Our number system has been developing for hundreds of years. The modern system we use today had many contributions from numerous countries and cultures (Reys et al., 2003).

There are four important features of the number system:

1. *Using place value.* The position of a numeral represents its value, for example, the numeral 2 in the numbers 21, 132, and 213 represents different ways of thinking about the value of the number 2. In the first example, 2 represents 2 tens or 20, the second 2 represents 2 ones or 2, and in the third case 2 represents 2 hundreds or 200.

2. *Base of ten.* Base in the number system means a collection. In our number system, ten is the value that determines a new collection. Our number system has ten numerals: 0, 1, 2, 3, 4, 5, 6, 7, 8, and 9. This collection is called a *base-ten system.*
3. *Use of zero.* Unlike other number systems, our system has a symbol for zero. Encourage students to think about the Roman numeral system. The reason it is so cumbersome to use today is that it has no zero.
4. *Additive property.* Our number system has a specific way of naming numbers. For example, the number 321 names the number 300 + 20 + 1.

Place value is one of the most important concepts in the elementary and middle school. Solving problems that involve computation includes understanding and expressing multi-digit numbers. Yet knowing when to exchange groups of ones for tens, or what to do with a zero in the hundreds place when subtracting, for example, confuses many students who, then, struggle with the step-by-step subtraction problem.

Students are helped by solving real-world problems with hands-on materials such as counters, base-ten blocks, and place value charts. Students must create meaning for themselves by using manipulatives (Kilpatrick, Swafford, & Findell, 2001).

The following place value activities are designed to get learners actively involved.

Grouping by Tens or Trading

Students need experiences in counting many objects, trading for groups of tens, hundreds, and thousands, and talking together about their findings. Students need many models. Bean sticks and base-ten blocks are two models widely used by teachers. But students also need piles of materials (rice, beans, straws, counters, and unifix cubes) to practice counting, grouping, and trading.

Ask students to group by tens as they work. This makes the task of counting easier for students; counting by tens also helps students check errors in their counting. But most importantly, sorting by tens shows students how large amounts of objects can be organized. Some common errors related to place value include not regrouping when necessary or regrouping in the wrong place (Kamii, 2000).

Trading Rules

The base-ten system works by trading ten ones for one ten, or the reverse; trading one ten for ten ones; ten tens for one hundred; ten hundreds for one thousand; and so on. Base-ten blocks are a great ready-made model in teaching this principle. Encourage students to make their own model. Building models with Popsicle sticks and lima beans works equally well.

Or, if teachers wish to have students use construction paper and scissors, students can make their base-ten models by cutting out small squares of paper and pasting them on a ten strip to form a ten. Then, after completing ten tens, paste the ten strips together to make a hundred, and then paste the hundreds together to form a thousand. It is time-consuming work but well worth the effort.

Proportional models such as base-ten blocks, bean sticks, and ten strips provide physical representation. In all the examples just mentioned, the material for ten is ten times the size of the unit; the hundred is ten times the size of the ten; the thousand is ten times the size of the hundred; and so on. Metric measurement provides another proportional model. A meter stick, decimeter rods, and centimeter cubes can be used to model any three-digit number.

Nonproportional models such as money do not exhibit a size relationship but rather present a practical real-life model. Because both types of models are important and should be used, we recommend starting students with proportional models, as they're more concrete and they can help learners understand the relationships more clearly.

Teaching Place Value

It is important that students think of numbers in many ways. A good place to start is to pass out a base-ten mat with the words "ones," "tens," and "hundreds." Also, pass out base-ten blocks to each of the students (units, longs, and flats). The units represent ones, longs represent tens, and flats represent hundreds.

Now, have the students build the number they hear. If, for example, the teacher says the number 42, the students take four long rods (tens) and place them on the tens column of their mat, and two units, placing them in the ones column. Encourage students to test their skill in a small group by thinking of a number, verbalizing it, and then checking other students' mats.

FRACTIONS

Fraction concepts are among the most complicated and important mathematical ideas that students encounter. Perhaps, because of their complexity, fractions are also among the least understood by students. Some of the difficulties may arise from the different ways of representing fractions: spoken symbols, written symbols, manipulative materials, pictures, and real-world situations.

It is difficult for struggling students to make sense of these different ways of representing fractions and connecting them in meaningful ways. Learners need many chances to work with concrete materials, observe and talk about fractional parts, and relate their experiences to science and mathematical notation. Three meanings of fractions—part-whole, quotient, and ratio—are found in most elementary and middle school programs.

Part-Whole Fraction Model

Most fraction ideas are based on the part-whole fraction meaning. The part-whole meaning of a fraction such as 3/5 indicates that a whole has been divided into 5 equal parts and 3 of those parts are being used. The fraction may be shown with a model.

_____ |///////| |///////| |///////| |_____|_____|

Fraction as a Quotient

The fraction 3/5 may also be looked at as a quotient 3 ÷ 5. This view also comes from dividing something. Imagine you had three big cookies. You want to divide the three cookies among five friends or 3 ÷ 5. How much would each of your friends get? Each person gets 1/5 + 1/5 + 1/5 or 3/5.

Fraction as a Ratio

The fraction 3/5 may also represent a ratio, such as there are three boys for every five girls.

Fraction as a Region

The region is the most concrete form of understanding a fraction. It is easily handled by students. The region is the whole and the parts are congruent (the same size and shape). The region may be any shape such as a circle, square, or triangle. A variety of shapes may be used so that students do not think that a fraction is always "part of a pizza."

Fraction as a Length

Any unit can be partitioned into fractional parts. A number line is a good example. Oftentimes, teachers use manipulatives such as fraction bars; one helpful activity along these lines is to have students make a fraction kit.

Make a Fraction Kit

This introductory activity introduces fractions to students. Fractions are presented as parts of a whole.

Materials.   Each student needs seven different 3″ × 18″ strips of colored construction paper, a pair of scissors, and an envelope to put their set of fraction pieces labeled as follows: 1, 1/2, 1/3, 1/4, 1/8, 1/12, and 1/16.

Directions.   Direct students to cut and label the strips as follows:

1. Have students select a colored strip. Emphasize that this strip represents one whole, and have students label the strip 1/1 or 1.
2. Ask students to choose another color, fold it in half, cut it, and then label each piece 1/2. Talk about what 1/2 means (1/2 means 1 piece out of 2 total pieces).
3. Have students select another color, and have them fold and cut it into four pieces, labeling each piece 1/4. Again, discuss what 1/4 means (1 piece out of 4 total pieces; compare the 4 pieces with the whole).
4. Have students fold, cut, and label a fourth colored strip into eighths, a fifth strip into twelfths, and a sixth strip into sixteenths.

Now, each student has a fraction kit. Encourage students to compare the sizes of the pieces and talk together about what they discover. For example, students can easily observe that the fractional piece 1/16 is smaller than the piece marked 1/4. This is a good time to introduce equivalent fractions.

- "How many 1/16 pieces would it take to equal 1/4?"
- "What other fractional pieces would equal 1/4?"

Explaining equivalence with a fraction kit makes fractions more meaningful (Burns, 2001).

Evaluation, Completion, and/or Follow-up

This follow-up section contains activities that engage students in the use of their fraction kit.

Activity 1: Fraction Cover-Up

Have students work in small groups. Have each student start with the 1 strip. Using the pieces from the fraction kit, challenge students to be the first to cover the whole strip completely. The game rules are as follows: have students take turns rolling the cube labeled with fractions. The fraction that is shown when the cube is rolled tells the students the size of the piece to place on the strip. When getting close to the end, students must roll exactly the fraction that is needed.

Activity 2: Fraction Equivalence Game

This game gives students opportunities to work with equivalent fractions. Each player starts with the 1 strip covered with two 1/2 fraction pieces. The challenge is to be the first to remove the strips completely. Encourage students to follow these rules. Students take turns rolling the fraction cube.

A student has three options on each turn: to remove a piece (only if he or she has a piece indicated by the fraction on the cube), to exchange any of the pieces left for equivalent pieces, or do nothing and pass the cube to the next player. A student may not remove a piece and trade in the same turn but can choose to do one or the other.

MEASUREMENT STANDARD

Concepts and skills in the measurement standard deal with making comparisons between what is being measured and a standard unit of measurement. Students acquire measuring skills through firsthand experiences. It is important to remind students that measurement is never exact; even the most careful measurements are approximations. Students need to learn to make estimates when measuring.

Measurement tools and skills have many uses in everyday life. Being able to measure connects mathematics to the real-world environment. Being able to use the tools of measurement (e.g., rulers, measuring cups, scales, thermometers, meter sticks, etc.) and to estimate with these tools are essential skills for students to develop.

Instruction in measurement should progress through these attributes of measurement: length, weight/mass, volume/capacity, time, temperature, and area. Within each of these areas, students need to begin making comparisons with standard and nonstandard units. In upper grades, more emphasis can be placed on using measurement tools to measure.

Sample Measurement Activity: Body Comparisons

Students need direct, concrete experiences when interacting with mathematical ideas. The following activities are designed to clarify many commonly held incorrect ideas.

Find the Ratio of Your Height to Your Head

How many times do you think a piece of string equal to your height would wrap around your head? Many students have a mental picture of their body, and they make a guess relying on that perception. Have students make an estimate, then have them verify it for themselves. Few make an accurate guess based on their perceptions.

Compare Height with Circumference

Have students imagine a soft drink can. Then, have them think about taking a string and wrapping it around the can to measure its circumference.
Have students guess if they think the circumference is longer, shorter, or
about the same height as the can. Encourage students to estimate how high
the circumference measure will reach. Then, have the students try it.

Like the previous activity, many students guess incorrectly. The common
misperception is that the string will be about the same length as the height
of the can. There is a feeling of surprise or mental confusion when they
discover that the circumference is about three times the height of the can.
Struggling students feel more confident when they see fellow classmates
searching for a correct answer. Repeat the experiment with other cylindri-
cal containers. Have students record their predictions and come up with a
conclusion (Burns, 2001).

Group Activity: Estimate, Measure, and Compare Your Shoes

Materials.   Unifix cubes, shoes.

Directions.   Estimate how many unifix cubes would fit in your shoe.
Write your estimate. Choose a volunteer from your group to take off his or
her shoe. Then, students are instructed to estimate how many unifix cubes
would fit in the shoe.

When finished with the estimate, have students actually measure the
shoe using unifix cubes. Students record the measurement. Pass the shoe to
the next group; they estimate and record the actual measurement. Continue
passing the shoes around the class until students have recorded estimates
and actual measurements of the shoes from each of the groups.

Evaluation.   Instruct students to compare the shoes. Have students
explain what attribute of measurement they used. Encourage students to
think of another way to measure the shoes. Explain how it might be more
accurate (Battista, 2002). Struggling students are actively engaged in estimating and measuring each other's shoes.

Pumpkin Measurement Lesson

Objectives

To have the class estimate the size, weight, and circumference of the class
pumpkins.

Materials

Unifix cubes.

Activity 1—Estimate the Height of the Pumpkin

Materials.   One pumpkin.
Directions

1. Place the pumpkin on a table in the room.
2. Make a poster with these questions and room for groups' estimates. How high is the pumpkin?
3. Have groups line up the unifix cubes on their desks. Next, instruct students to guess the number of cubes they think will be equal to the pumpkin's height.
4. Direct groups to write their name on the poster in the front of the room. Ask them to write their estimate on the poster.
5. Then, have the groups measure the pumpkin by counting the unifix cubes. Ask them to write in their portfolio their estimate and how many unifix cubes they used.

Activity 2—Estimating the Pumpkin's Weight

Materials.   One pumpkin, a scale, and two books.
Directions

1. Instruct students to hold the first book to feel how much three pounds is.
2. Now, have them hold the pumpkin. Does it weigh the same as the three-pound book? More or less? Does it weigh as much as two books? How much would that be? Repeat with the lighter, one-pound book and the pumpkin. Ask similar questions.
3. Have groups record their estimates on the class chart.
4. To measure how much the pumpkin weighs, place it gently on the scale and have students record the number.

Follow-up.   Groups read the estimate chart to see who is the closest.

Activity 3—Estimating Circumference of the Pumpkin

Materials.   One pumpkin, string, and scissors.
Directions

1. Using a string and scissors, instruct groups to cut three strips of string to the length they think would go around the pumpkin's waist.
2. Have groups measure their string estimate (number of inches).
3. Next, have groups hang their string from the chart under their group's marker.

Follow-up.   Groups, then, actually measure the circumference of the pumpkin. Students check the estimation chart to compare accuracy.

PROBLEM-SOLVING STANDARD

Problem solving has been central to mathematics education for decades. Problem solving refers to engaging in a task where the solution is not known. George Polya, a well-known mathematician, devised a four-step scheme for solving problems: understand the problem, create a plan or strategy, follow through with the approach selected, and check back. Does it make sense?

Problems are teaching tools that can be used for different purposes. The solutions are never routine, and there is usually no right answer because of the multitude of possibilities. Strategies include guessing and checking, making a chart or table, drawing a picture, acting out the problem, working backward, creating a simpler problem, looking for patterns, using an equation, using logic, asking someone for help, making an organized list, using a computer simulation, or coming up with one's own idea. Take a risk.

Nothing has more strength than dire necessity.

—Euripides[5]

Teachers should model the problem-solving strategies needed for thinking about mathematics content or responding to particular math problems. Modeling might include the thinking that goes into selecting what strategy to use, deciding what options are possible, and checking on their progress as they go along. Reluctant learners can catch on quickly if guided through this process. The following are a few problem-solving activities.

Present Interesting Problems

Present a problem to the class. Have students draw pictures of what the problem is about, act out the problem, or have one student read the problem leaving out the numbers. Once students begin to visualize what the problem is about, they have much less difficulty solving it. Students should work in small groups when arriving at strategies and when solving the problems. Students should write down how they solved it and discuss and check their answers with other groups.

The following is a sample problem to present to the class.

Solve This Problem

One day Farmer Bill was counting his pigs and chickens.
He noticed they had 60 legs and there were 22 animals in all.
How many of each kind of animal did he have?

This is a fun problem for struggling students if they can draw a picture of the animals and think about what the problem is asking.

Record Your Strategy Below

Solve the Problem Another Way

List the standards used.

TEACHING BASIC FACTS

When students are learning about the operations of addition and subtraction, it is helpful for them to make connections between these processes and the world around them. Story problems help them see the actions of joining and separating. Using manipulative and sample word problems gives them experiences in joining sets and figuring out the differences between them. By pretending and using concrete materials, learning becomes more meaningful. Tell stories in which the learners pretend to be animals or things. Representing ideas and connecting them to mathematics is the basis for understanding. Representations make mathematics more concrete. A typical elementary classroom has several sets of manipulative materials to improve computational skills and make learning more enjoyable.

Base-ten blocks will be used in these activities to represent the sequence of moving from concrete manipulations to the abstract algorithms. Students need many chances to become familiar with the blocks, discovering the vocabulary (ones = units, tens = longs, hundreds = flats) and the relationships among the pieces. The following activities will explore trading relationships in addition, subtraction, multiplication, and division.

The Banker's Game (Simple Addition)

In this activity, small groups of students will be involved in representing tens. The game works best dividing the class into small groups (four or five players and one banker). Each player begins with a playing board divided into units, longs, and flats. Before beginning, the teacher should explain the use of the board. Any blocks the student receives should be placed on the board in the column that has the same shape at the top.

A student begins the game by rolling a die and asking the banker for the number rolled in *units*. They are then placed in the units column on the student's board. Each student is in charge of checking her or his board to decide if a trade is possible. The trading rule states that no player may have more than nine objects in any column at the end of her or his turn. If the player has more than nine, he or she must gather them together and go to the banker to make a trade (e.g., ten units for one long).

Play does not proceed to the next player until all the trades have been made. The winner is the first player to earn five tens. This game can be modified by using two dice and increasing the winning amount.

The Take Away Game (Subtraction)

This game is simply the reverse of the Banker's Game. The emphasis here is on representing the regrouping of tens. Players must give back in units to the bank whatever is rolled on the die. To begin, all players place the same number of blocks on their boards. Exchanges must be made with the banker. Rules are quickly made by the students (e.g., when rolling a six, a player may hand the banker a long and ask for four units back).

It is helpful for students to explain their reasoning to one another. The winner is the first to have an empty playing board. Students should decide in their group beforehand whether an exact roll is necessary to go out or not.

Teaching Division with Understanding

Base-ten blocks bring understanding to an often complex algorithmic process. The following activity is a good place to start when introducing and representing division.

1. Using base-ten blocks, have students show 393 with flats, rods, and units.
2. Have the students divide the blocks into three equal piles.
3. Slowly, ask students to explain what they did. How many flats in each pile, how many rods, and how many units?
4. Give students several more problems. Here are examples: Start with 435 and divide into three piles. Encourage students to explain how many flats, rods, and units they found at the end of all their exchanges. In this problem, one flat will have to be exchanged for 10 rods (tens), and then the rods divided into three groups. One rod remains.

   Next, students will have to exchange the one rod for ten units, and then divide the units into three groups. No units are left in this problem. Continue doing more verbal problems, pausing and letting students explain how they solved them. What exchanges were made? It is helpful to have students work together trying to explain their reasoning, correcting each other, and asking questions.
5. After many problems, perhaps at the next class session, explain to the students that they're now ready to record their work on paper still using the blocks.

a. The teacher then shows two ways to write the problem.

$$435 \div 3 = \text{and } 3/435.$$

b. Then, the teacher asks the students three questions and waits until all students have finished with each question.

   Question 1: How many hundreds in each group? (Students go to their record sheet above the division symbol of the problem. They answer one flat, so they record 1 on their sheet.)

   Question 2: How many in all? Students check how many cubes are represented, they answer 300, and they record 300 on their sheet.

   Question 3: How many are left? Students return to the problem and subtract 435 - 300 = 135.

   Now, the problem continues with the tens, then the ones. Again, they start over asking the three questions each time (Burns, 1988).

6. For advanced students, this seems like an elaborate way of doing division. By using manipulative methods and teaching with understanding, beginning division makes sense to elementary students. Teachers can introduce shortcuts later to make more advanced division easier and faster.

Students learn best when they are actively engaged in meaningful mathematics tasks using hands-on materials. Such a mathematics classroom encourages students' thinking, risk taking, and communicating with peers and adults about everyday experiences.

SAMPLE ACTIVITIES

In an effort to link the mathematics standards to classroom practice, a few sample activities are presented. The intent is not to prescribe an activity for a unique grade level but rather to offer innovative activities that could be modified and used in many grades.

Estimate and Compare

Objectives

In grades K–4, the curriculum includes estimation so students can

- explore estimation strategies;
- recognize when an estimate is appropriate;
- determine the reasonableness of results; and
- apply estimation in working with quantities, measurement, computation, and problem solving.

Math and science instruction in the primary grades tries to make classifying and using numerals an essential part of classroom experience. Learners need many opportunities to identify quantities and see relationships between objects. Students count and write numerals. When developing beginning concepts, students need to manipulate concrete materials and relate numbers to problem situations (Greenes et al., 2004).

Individuals benefit by talking, writing, and hearing what others think. In the following activity, students are actively involved in estimating, manipulating objects, counting, verbalizing, writing, and comparing.

Directions

1. Divide students into small groups (two or three students). Place a similar group of objects in a color-coded container for each group. Pass out recording sheets divided into partitions with the color of the container in each box.
2. Have young students examine the container on their desks, estimate how many objects are present, discuss with their group, and write their guess next to the color on the sheet.
3. Next, have the group count the objects and write the number they counted next to the first number. Instruct the students to circle the greater number.
4. Switch cans or move to the next station and repeat the process. A variety of objects (small plastic cats, marbles, paper clips, colored shells, etc.) add interest and are real motivators.

Adding and Subtracting in Everyday Situations

Objectives

In the early grades, the mathematics curriculum should include concepts of addition and subtraction of whole numbers so that students can

- develop meaning for the operations by modeling and discussing a rich variety of problem situations; and
- relate the mathematical language and symbolism of operations to problem situations and informal language.

When students are learning about the operations of addition and subtraction, it's helpful for them to make connections between these processes and the world around them. Story problems using ideas from science and technology help them see the actions of joining and separating. Using manipulatives and sample word problems gives them experiences in joining sets and figuring out the differences between them. By pretending and using concrete materials, learning becomes more meaningful.

Directions

1. Divide students into small groups (two or three students).
2. Tell stories in which the learners can pretend to be animals, plants, other students, or even space creatures.
3. Telling stories is enhanced by having students use unifix cubes or other manipulatives to represent the people, objects, or animals in the oral problems.
4. Have students work on construction paper or prepare counting boards on which trees, oceans, trails, houses, space stations, and other things have been drawn.

NEW IDEAS ON TEACHING, LEARNING, AND ASSESSMENT

There is general agreement that a constructive, active view of learning must be reflected in the way that math and science are taught (Van De Walle, 2004). Classroom mathematics experiences should stimulate students, build on past understandings, and explore their own ideas. This means that students have many chances to interpret math ideas and construct understandings for themselves.

To do this, students need to be involved in problem-solving investigations and projects that engage thinking and reasoning. Working with materials in a group situation helps reinforce thinking. Students talk together, present their understandings, and try to make sense of the task. Students reflect on and evaluate their work.

Some of the newest methods for teaching mathematics in active small group situations include writing about how they solved problems, keeping daily logs or journals, and expressing attitudes through creative endeavors such as building or art work (Whitin & Whitin, 2000). Rarely does a problem become completely exhausted, so the understanding of a solution can always be improved. Comprehending links and making thoughtful connections are important tools in the effort to go beyond the given to see context, patterns, and relationships.

With the renewed emphasis on thinking, communicating, and making connections between topics, students are more in control of their learning. With collaborative inquiry, students have many experiences with manipulatives, calculators, and computers, and working on real-world applications.

There are more opportunities to make connections and work with peers on interesting problems. The ability to express basic math understandings, estimate confidently, and check the reasonableness of their estimates is part of what it means to be literate, numerate, and employable.

Whether it's making sense of newspaper graphs, identifying the dangers of global warming, or reading schedules at work, mathematics has real meaning in our lives. The same might be said for using the calculator, working with paper and pencil, or doing mental mathematics. Students must master the basic facts of arithmetic before they can harness the full power of mathematics. Unfortunately, simply learning to do algorithms (the step-by-step procedures used to compute with numbers) will not ensure success with problems that demand reasoning ability.

The good news is that, across the country, the curriculum trend is toward making mathematics more interactive and relevant to what students need to know in order to meet changing intellectual and societal demands. And, it is doing this without dropping the underlying structure of mathematics.

Teachers have found that the more opportunities students have to participate with others, the more likely they are to learn to do mathematics in knowledgeable and meaningful ways. Quite simply, students learn more if they have opportunities to describe their own ideas, listen to others, and cooperatively solve problems. All collaborative or cooperative learning structures are designed to increase student participation in learning, while building on the twin incentives of shared group goals and individual accountability.

HELPING STUDENTS HAVE SUCCESS IN MATHEMATICS

- Introduce math ideas in real-world settings.
- Teach an understanding of the math operations (adding, subtracting, multiplying, and dividing) by arousing their natural curiosity.
- Use differentiated instruction to allow for students' learning styles.
- Integrate ideas with the mathematics standards.
- Plan exciting lessons.
- Rewrite textbook materials to accommodate learners' interests.
- Allow students to explore materials before they use them.
- Access innovative ideas on teaching mathematics plus activities and resources.

How do you know if your solution to a problem is correct if you haven't proven it? When it comes to mathematical problem solving, have students ask each other for proof when an individual or a team comes up with an answer. Encourage students to go beyond equating proof with *what is true*; it's best to think of "proof" as showing *why*.

SUMMARY AND CONCLUSION

Helping students discover their personal voice, strengths, and interests is central to generating creativity and innovative behavior. In a differentiated math classroom, teachers stress investigations and problem solving. They also use small group activities that are designed to interest a wide range of students.

An important part of the approach is making available a wide range of choices to learners and giving them the power to make decisions whenever possible. Problem solving, communication, collaborative learning, deductive reasoning, and making connections are all part of what thoughtful math instruction is about.

The future belongs to the nation that best educates its citizens. Being naive or afraid of a subject as important as mathematics can be a real problem in school, in the workplace, and in a democratic society. It is also a problem if students don't understand how math impacts their day-to-day lives. Experienced math teachers know that each student has a different understanding of math-related issues and that each learning task presents its own set of challenges.

They also know that a lot can be accomplished by working on a wide range of problems together. In fact, student learning teams are a proven and powerful way to approach innovative mathematics instruction. Peer support helps students feel more confident and more willing to take the kind of risks that go hand in hand with creativity and innovation.

As teachers go about matching math lessons to the readiness, interests, and talents of individual learners (i.e., differentiation), the result is likely to be the development of a natural sense of community in the classroom. This can help provide helpful social support for recognizing the relationship of mathematical problems to life outside of school.

Another benefit in linking instruction to the world outside of school is that students will be stimulated to identify problems they would be interested in solving collaboratively. Along the way, learners may well be motivated to become more thoughtful and considerate individuals as they cooperate in pairs or small groups.

In addition to improving the education of children, we must all take more responsibility for improving our own education. As teachers, it is time to expect more from ourselves and from our students. Good teachers of mathematics generate students' confidence in their ability to understand and apply the subject and become mathematically empowered. They frequently stimulate creative and innovative thinking by taking care to value the students' own ideas. The ultimate goal is helping students stir their imaginations to gain an appreciation of the power, beauty, and fascination of mathematics.

All science requires mathematics. The knowledge of mathematical things is almost innate in us. This is the easiest of sciences, a fact which is obvious in that no one's brain rejects it; for laymen and people who are utterly illiterate know how to count and reckon.

—Roger Bacon[6]

REFERENCES

Adams, T. (2000). Helping children learn mathematics through multiple intelligences and standards for school mathematics. *Childhood Education, 77,* 86–92.

Battista, M. T. (2002). Learning in an inquiry-based classroom. In J. Sowder & B. Schappelle (Eds.), *Lessons learned from research* (pp. 75–84). Reston, VA: NCTM.

Benjamin, A. (2003). *Differentiated instruction: A guide for elementary school teachers.* Larchmont, NY: Eye on Education.

Burns, M. (2001). *About teaching mathematics: A K–8 resource.* White Plains, NY: Math Solutions Publication.

Burns, M. (1988). *Mathematics with manipulatives* (six videotapes). White Plains, NY: Cuisinaire Company of America.

Craft, A. (2005). *Creativity in the schools: Tensions and dilemmas.* New York: Routledge.

Dixon-Krauss, L. (1996). *Vygotsky in the classroom.* Boston: Allyn & Bacon.

Greenes, C. E., Dacey, L., Cavanagh, M., Findell, C. R., Sheffield, L. J., & Small, M. (2004). *Navigating through problem solving and reasoning in prekindergarten-kindergarten (principles and standards for school mathematics navigations).* Reston, VA: NCTM.

Kamii, C. (2000). *Young children reinvent arithmetic: Implications of Piaget's theory.* New York: Teacher's College Press.

Kilpatrick, J., Swafford, J., & Findell, B. (Eds.). (2001). *Adding it up: Helping children learn mathematics.* Washington, DC: National Academy Press.

National Council of Teachers of Mathematics (NCTM). (2000). *Principles and standards for school mathematics.* Reston, VA: NCTM.

Reys, R., Lindquist, M., Lamdin, D., Smith, N., & Suydam, M. (2003). *Helping children learn mathematics.* New York: John Wiley & Sons.

Stephen, M., Bowers, J., Cobb, P., & Gravemeijer, K. (2004). *Supporting students' development of measuring conceptions: Analyzing students' learning in social context.* Reston, VA: NCTM.

Van De Walle, J. (2004). *Elementary and middle school mathematics: Thinking developmentally* (5th ed.). Boston: Pearson Education.

White, D. (2004). By way of introduction: Teaching mathematics to special needs students. *Teaching Children Mathematics, 11* (3), 116–117.

Whitin, P., & Whitin, D. (2000). *Math is language too: Talking and writing in the mathematics classroom.* Reston, VA: NCTM. Urbana, IL: National Council of Teachers of English.

RESOURCES AND SUGGESTED READINGS

Cavanagh, M., Dacey, L., Findell, C., Greenes, C., Sheffield, L., & Small, M. (2004). *Navigating through number and operations in prekindergarten–grade 2*. Reston, VA: NCTM.

Friedman, T. (2007). *The world is flat: A brief history of the twenty-first century*. New York: Picador.

Lewin, T. (2006, November 14). As math scores lag, a new push for the basics. *New York Times*.

Polya, G. (1957). *How to solve it* (2nd ed.). Princeton, NJ: Princeton University Press.

Smutny, J., & von Fremd, S. (2009). *Igniting creativity in gifted learners, K–6: Strategies for every teacher*. Thousand Oaks, CA: Corwin Press.

4

Science Inquiry

Thinking, Differentiation, and Preparing for the Future

> The future will always be different, not just from what we imagine, but what we can imagine
>
> —Ian McDonald[1]

Science forces us to change ourselves by constantly making us think and rethink what we know. It also teaches us to value both the facts and the imagination's ability to come up with new findings and insights. Science doesn't just focus on what is likely because that would diminish the sense of surprise and wonder that comes from making unexpected discoveries about the natural world.

In the classroom, inquiry is the process that most of today's students use to learn about science. It involves asking questions and engaging in a systematic search for answers. Reasoning, feelings, and the exploration of new ideas are all part of the inquiry process.

Science is a body of knowledge and a process that leads to a way of knowing or constructing reality. In this chapter, we will explore the innovative nature of science, provide an overview of the science standards, and point to the implications for differentiated instruction (DI).

It is our belief that intellectual tools like inquiry can help build creative and innovative capacity across the curriculum. Sample activities, teaching methods, and DI techniques are introduced in a way that encourages the incorporation of scientific inquiry into every aspect of classroom life. We also point to the power that mathematics and technology bring to the nature of the scientific enterprise.

Along the science literacy glide path, inquiry frequently involves the critical and creative uses of scientific knowledge. Inquiry also encourages science-related attitudes that connect to the processes of science. It is important to make sure that all students have the opportunity to learn about scientific methods and become science literate (Victor, Kellough, & Tai, 2008).

The National Science Education Standards (NSES) point to the need for a scientifically literate citizenry. They go on to emphasize teaching the processes of science and paying close attention to cognitive abilities. Successful science inquiry lessons help students understand logic, while gaining a respect for evidence and extending knowledge to construct explanations of natural phenomena.

The science standards and just about every district and state curriculum also suggest that inquiry is the cornerstone of good science teaching. There is general agreement that science literacy should begin in the early grades, where students are naturally curious and eager to explore.

Another point of agreement is that science learning, at its best, is an active process. Throughout this dynamic process, students ask questions, make predictions, design investigations, collect and analyze data, make products, and share ideas (Krajcik & Czerniak, 2007). As the standards suggest, getting students actively involved in the process of actually *doing* science leads them to greater scientific awareness and the frontiers of twenty-first-century innovation.

Teachers at all grade levels are now expected to be able to plan and implement inquiry-based science lessons and science programs. In the most successful science programs, teachers pay attention to the what and how of teaching—refining and adding to what they already know.

TEACHERS, INQUIRY, AND THE NATIONAL SCIENCE EDUCATION STANDARDS

The most effective teachers have built up their science knowledge base and developed a repertoire of current pedagogical techniques. They are familiar with both the subject matter *and* the characteristics of effective instruction. Collaborative learning groups and a variety of questioning and discovery learning strategies can teach students science in an effective yet creative way.

By focusing on real investigations and participatory learning, it is possible to move students from the concrete to the abstract as they explore themes that connect science, math, and technology. It's all part of preparing the next generation of thoughtful citizen innovators.

Inquiry is more than hands-on activities; it is dependent on a set of interrelated processes guided by questions. It is a place where students collaborate and experience things for themselves. Skills related to creativity, ingenuity, and innovation are close associates of scientific inquiry (Saracho & Spodek, 2008).

Children and young adults are very inquisitive, so encouraging that inherent trait will provide lifelong skills in solving practical problems. Observing, measuring, collecting, and classifying are some of the other attributes of scientific inquiry that come naturally to many students. In addition to these elements, good science lessons frequently encourage problem solving, questioning, examining sources of information, forming explanations, and communicating conclusions.

Wanting to make sense of the world is a natural motivator that leads students to inquire, discover, and understand the world they're in. An active science curriculum has the power to make a difference in the lives of students and in the society where they live. Changes in science education have a lot to do with the changing nature of science itself. For example, scientific research no longer strictly limits itself to theories and discoveries about the natural world.

Scientists now pay more attention to finding solutions to science-related social, economic, and personal problems. Health, energy, technology, and the environment are getting more attention than ever.

Suggestions from the NSE Standards

1. Have broader depth and less superficial coverage.
2. Focus on inquiry and problem solving.
3. Provide different ways for students to learn.
4. Have a common core of subject matter for all students.
5. Emphasize the skills, knowledge, and importance of science.
6. Provide closer links between science, math, technology, and creative habits.
7. Create an integrated science curriculum that is attuned to personal relevance.

One of the changes from the traditional curriculum is adding depth to the content of the science curriculum. Less really can be more if you focus in depth and if you take more time to teach fewer skills and concepts. It can lead to greater understanding and retention. The science curriculum offers a common core of subject matter. A common curriculum for all students draws students together, while a fragmented curriculum such as tracking separates students based on ability or career goals. In responding to individual differences, the common curriculum leads to unity and builds character among students.

Whether it is in or out of school, math and technology are keys to scientific inquiry. Ideally, the various developmental levels of science are coordinated so that what's taught in the third-grade science builds on the second-grade content and leads to the fourth-grade science curriculum.

The reality is that students move, the school staff shifts around, students fail to learn, and some teachers do as little science instruction as possible. The end result is that, in any given grade level, the science background of students is going to be all over the developmental map. That's where DI comes into its own.

DI is not so much a teaching model as it is a way of teaching and learning that starts where individuals *are*, rather than assuming they are at some prescribed level. What matter most are student readiness, interest, and learning profile.

In the differentiated classroom, teaching is targeted to the varying learning needs of diverse students. Doing collaborative work with a partner or in a small group is a good way to deal with student learning differences. This can be done while still making sure that all students are engaged in high-quality scientific inquiry (Renzulli & Reis, 2008).

DIFFERENTIATED LEARNING STRATEGIES

Many DI strategies are based on the idea that teachers can adapt instruction to student differences. To reach all students, teachers have to provide the right level of challenge for students who perform below grade level, for gifted students, and for everyone in between. This means working to deliver instruction in ways that meet the differing needs of auditory, visual, and kinesthetic learners, while trying to connect to students' personal interests.

Tips for Differentiating Instruction

1. Apply a Collaborative Approach

Collaborative learning is a "total class" approach that lends itself to differentiated instruction. It requires everyone to think, learn, and teach. Within a collaborative learning classroom, there will be many and varied strengths among students.

Every student will possess characteristics that lend themselves to enriching learning for all students. Sometimes, these "differences" may constitute a conventionally defined "disability"; sometimes, it simply means the inability to do a certain life or school-related task. And sometimes, it means, as with the academically talented, being capable of work well beyond the norm. Within the collaborative learning classroom, such exceptionality need not constitute a handicap.

Collaborative learning is not simply a technique that a teacher can just select and adopt in order to "accommodate" a student within the classroom. Making significant change in the classroom process requires that teachers undergo changes in the ways that they teach and in the ways they view students. This means creating comfortable, yet challenging, learning environments rich in diversity. The goal is collaboration among all types of learners. In mixed-ability groups, the emphasis must be on proficiency rather than age or grade level as a basis for student progress.

Active collaboration requires a depth of planning, a redefinition of planning, testing, and classroom management. Perhaps, most significantly, collaborative learning values individual abilities, talents, skills, and background knowledge.

2. Form Multi-age Flexible Groups

To maximize the potential of each learner, educators need to meet each student at his or her starting point and ensure substantial growth during each school term. Classrooms that respond to student differences benefit virtually all students. Being flexible in grouping students gives students many options to develop their particular strengths and show their performance.

3. Set Up Learning Centers

A learning center is a space in the class that contains a group of activities or materials designed to teach, reinforce, or extend a particular concept. Centers generally focus on an important topic; use materials and activities addressing a wide range of reading levels, learning profiles, and student interests.

A teacher may create many centers, such as a science center, a music center, or a reading center. Students don't need to move to all of them at once to achieve competence with a topic or a set of skills. Have students rotate among the centers. Learning centers generally include activities that range from simple to complex.

Effective learning centers usually provide clear directions for students including what a student should do if he or she completes a task, or what to do if they need help. A record-keeping system should be included to monitor what students do at the center. An ongoing assessment of student growth in the class should be in place, which can lead to teacher adjustments in center tasks.

4. Develop Tiered Activities

These are helpful strategies when teachers want to address students with different learning needs. For example, a student who struggles with reading from a science textbook or has a difficult time with complex vocabulary needs some help in trying to make sense of the important ideas in a given chapter. At the same time, a student who is advanced well beyond grade level needs to find a genuine challenge in working with the same concepts.

Teachers use tiered activities so that all students focus on necessary understandings and skills but at different levels of complexity and abstractness. By keeping the focus of the activities the same but providing different routes of access, the teacher maximizes the likelihood that each student comes away with important skills and is appropriately challenged.

Teachers should select the concepts and skills that will be the focus of the activity for all learners. Using assessments to find out what the students need and creating an interesting activity that will cause learners to use an important skill or understand a key idea is part of the tiered approach. It is important to provide varying materials and activities. Teachers match a version of the task to each student based on student needs and task requirements. The goal is to match the task's degree of difficulty and the students' readiness.

5. Make Learning More Challenging

Challenging strategies put more emphasis on authentic problems where students are encouraged to formulate their own problems on a topic in which they're interested and work together to solve it. Problems are connected to the "real world" and allow time for discussion and sharing of ideas among students.

6. Have a Clear Set of Standards

Integrating standards into the curriculum helps make learning more meaningful and interesting to reluctant learners. Having a clearly defined set of standards helps teachers concentrate on instruction and makes clear to students the expectations of the class. Students come to understand what is expected and work collaboratively to achieve it. Challenging collaborative groups to help each other succeed is another way to avoid poor performance.

7. Expand Learning Options

Not all students learn in the same way or at the same time. Teachers can expand learning options by differentiating instruction. This means teachers need to reach out to struggling students or small groups to improve teaching in order to create the best learning experience possible.

8. Introduce Active Reading Strategies

There is an approach which uses "active reading" strategies to improve students' abilities to explain difficult text. This step-by-step process involves reading aloud to yourself or someone else as a way to build science understandings. Although most learners self-explain without verbalizing, the active reading approach is similar to that used by anyone attempting to master new material. The best way to truly learn is to teach or to explain something to someone else. You could go over it with someone online.

There are good examples of how Web-based inquiry can help connect scientific investigations to real-world problems and assist in helping students understand the beauty and the utility of science (Slotta & Linn, 2009). But face-to-face communication is usually best because, for one thing, many online/text users won't send *or* respond to anything longer than a brief text message.

Classroom teachers have to put tight controls on technological distractions to build on the true social nature of learning. But let's face it—students of all ages may occasionally Tweet, Facebook, Google, FriendFeed, Digg, and search when the teacher isn't looking. Although it's called communication and social networking, Twitter (a micro-blogging site), texting, and all of their associates are threatening to turn face-to-face conversation into a lost art.

They may be nice to know about, but like e-mail, too much time with them can drive you to be "mad, bad, and dangerous to know." When the measure of a relationship is how quickly you respond to a five-word message, social interaction loses its impact. As human communication becomes more simplistic and sterile, we know more people more shallowly.

It's the same old story—technological change makes society more efficient and less personal. New ways of communicating can serve as an escape from real human interaction, with its rough edges, immediacy, and spontaneity. Marshall McLuhan said that new media changes the way we relate to each other and our communities.[2] Unfortunately, he may be right.

Take the example of e-mails giving us a superficial way of interacting with a lot of people along an avenue so narrow that deep human contact is nearly impossible. The landscape of e-mail is full of noise and imagined signals. Still, some of the technological possibilities have the potential of developing in a way that accommodates human nature. School should be a place where students at least have the possibility of getting away from technological distractions so they can experience the social nature of face-to-face learning.

In the classroom, much of the communication must be real conversation in the actual presence of others; this can make it more meaningful, immediate, imaginative, and spontaneous. Students need to know that scientific knowledge and authentic communication fuel human progress, but it's usually lack of imagination that gets in the way or puts on the brakes.

To use and understand science today requires an awareness of the nature of scientific endeavor and how it relates to our culture and our lives. It also requires learners who can tap into personal reservoirs of creativity in a way that helps them reach for original ideas. Scientific inquiry encourages the whole process because it involves intellectual curiosity, observation, posing questions, and actively seeking thoughtful answers.

THE NATIONAL SCIENCE CONTENT STANDARDS

Science instruction is now much more than the traditional textbook approach. Among other things, it's more differentiated, active, and collaborative.

The science standards suggest students should know, understand, and be able to do the following:

- understand the basic concepts and processes in science
- use the process of inquiry when doing science
- apply the properties of the physical, life, earth, and space sciences when doing activity-based learning
- use science understandings to design solutions to problems
- understand the connection of science and technology
- examine and practice science from personal and social viewpoints
- identify with the history and nature of science through readings, discussions, observations, and writings (National Research Council [NRC], 2000)

Getting everything right (all the time) in science instruction is unrealistic. So, it is little wonder that some science educators seem to be warming up to Voltaire's saying: "The perfect is the enemy of the good."[3] After all, there are times when a 75 percent solution now is better than a 100 percent solution later.

Inquiry, Science Standards, and the Process Skills

The inquiry skills of science are acquired through a questioning process; along the way, inquiry raises new questions and directions for examination. What students find often generates new ideas and suggests connections or ways of expressing concepts and interrelationships more clearly. The process of inquiry also helps students grow in content knowledge and the processes and skills of the search. It also invites unmotivated learners to explore anything that interests them. Regardless of the problem, subject, or issue, approaching inquiry with enthusiasm and care involves using thinking processes similar to those used by scientists.

Inquiry processes form a foundation of understanding and are components of the basic goals and standards of science and mathematics. These goals are intertwined and multidisciplinary, providing students with many opportunities to become involved in inquiry. Each goal involves one or more processes (or investigations).

The inquiry-process approach includes the major process skills and standards as outlined in the activities that follow. The science activities also include the key principles of a differentiated classroom. This includes the *content* (what students will learn), the *process* (the activities by which students make sense of important ideas using necessary skills), the *product* (how students show what they have learned and prove their point), and the *learning environment* (safe, comfortable conditions that set the tone for learning) (Tomlinson, Brimijoin & Narvaez, 2008).

SCIENCE ACTIVITIES BASED ON
THE SCIENCE STANDARDS

This section connects the science standards to elementary and middle school classrooms. The importance of establishing activities that use the inquiry skills of observing, measuring, recording data, and drawing reasonable conclusions are all emphasized. Whenever possible, mathematics is included in activities so that math and science skills are developed together.

Careful attention has been given to the sequence of activities within each section; the more general introductory activities come first, followed by more focused activities that build on each other to develop student understanding. At the end of each activity, suggestions for differentiated instruction are offered. These ideas provide a view of the differentiated process so that teachers can try out some differentiated strategies with their students.

Activity 1: Buttons and Shells (Grades K–5)

Inquiry Skills

Observing, classifying, comparing, sequencing, solving problems, group work, communicating, recording, gathering data, and measuring.

Science Standards

Inquiry, physical science, science and technology, personal perspectives, and written communications.

Description

In this introductory activity, students are observing by looking at the details of an object very closely. Students collect evidence by classifying, comparing, sequencing, gathering data, and trying to solve problems. Students communicate and work in groups to arrive at a solution.

New Vocabulary

Sorting, seriation, gradation, and Venn diagrams.

Materials

Bags of assorted buttons (one for each group), yarn or string dividers, and bags of small sea shells (one for each group).

Problem 1

How many ways can you sort your bag of buttons? Try to sort them at least ten different ways.

Problem 2

Make a Venn diagram using your bag of buttons. A Venn diagram is a method of illustrating set unions and intersections, for example, a set of blue buttons is one category; a set of round buttons is another category. A set of blue, round buttons is an intersecting category.

Problem 3

Classify the shells by seriation: light to dark (color), small to large, number of ridges, and amount of water the shell can hold.

Suggestions for Differentiating Instruction

The students work in groups to sort and classify the buttons ten different ways. The teacher differentiates learning materials making sure students can classify, sort, and find as many ways as possible. The teacher adapts instruction when students are about to create a Venn diagram and wants students to have as many chances as possible to find patterns, make comparisons, and figure out what intersection means. By modeling examples, the teacher helps students distinguish what is alike and different, and encourages partnerships that build success.

Activity 2: Unknown Liquids: Experiment (Grade 3 and Up)

Inquiry Skills

Hypothesizing, experimenting, and communicating.

Science Standards

Inquiry, physical science, science and technology, personal perspectives, and written communications.

Description

In this exploring activity students are experimenting with chemicals and doing physical science work. They are learning to use tools found in the lab and to know the safety rules of science, mathematics, and technology.

Materials for Each Table

    5 plastic containers
    5 liquids (oil, water, soap, alcohol, and vinegar)
    5 medicine droppers
    1 beaker
    1 small plastic beaker
    1 tray
    1 sheet of plastic wrap
    1 sheet of aluminum foil
    1 sheet of waxed paper

Procedures

1. Set up the containers with liquids.
2. Discuss the colored liquids.
3. Set up the trays with papers and materials for each group (5 eye droppers, 2 beakers, and 1 small plastic container).
4. On the board, list some possible experiments with liquids:
    - liquid races
    - floatability
    - density

- mixing liquids
- other ideas?

Problem

Try to discover what the four liquids are.

Rules

1. Each liquid is a household substance that may or may not have been colored with food coloring to hide its identity.
2. Students are limited to using only their sense of sight to do this experiment. Students should experiment by manipulating the liquids.
3. For safety reasons, caution students they are not to smell, touch, or taste the chemicals.
4. Each medicine dropper may be used to pick up only one liquid. We do not want contamination!

Group Task

Try to find out what the four unknown liquids are.

1. Write a description of the activity.
2. Explain how the group went about solving the problem.
3. Write what the group learned from the activity.
4. Provide some follow-up suggestions of how the activity could be improved or give suggestions of what to do after the activity is finished.

Suggestions for Differentiating Instruction

The students work together to try to figure out what the unknown liquids are. The teacher encourages a collaborative approach and offers suggestions on ways students can apply the knowledge of what they know about common chemicals. The teacher suggests

- testing different variables such as dropping a chemical on each sheet of paper to see how the papers react to the chemicals;
- shaking the containers with the liquids;
- trying some possible experiments; and
- observing, testing, being creative in your approach.

Activity 3: Looking at the Behavior of Molecules (Grades 3–6)

Inquiry Skills

Observing, comparing, hypothesizing, experimenting, and communicating.

Science Standards

Inquiry, physical science, science and technology, personal perspectives, and written communications.

Background Information Description

This activity simulates how molecules are connected to each other and the effect of temperature change on molecules. Students usually have questions about the way things work. Questions students naturally ask are the following: "Why does ice cream melt? "Why does the tea kettle burn my hand?" "Where does steam come from?" and "Why is it so difficult to break rocks?" Explain that molecules and atoms are the building blocks of matter. Heat and cold energy can change molecular form. The class is then asked to participate in the "hands-on" demonstration of how molecules work.

This is a great opportunity for students to participate and, perhaps, assume leadership as a group leader. Before beginning the demonstration, explain that matter and energy exist and can be changed but not created or destroyed. Ask for volunteers to role play the parts of molecules. Direct students to join hands showing how molecules are connected to each other, explaining that these connections represent matter in a solid form.

Next, ask them to "show what happens when a solid becomes a liquid." Heat causes the molecules to move more rapidly so they no longer can hold together. Students should drop hands and start to wiggle and move around. The next question is "How do you think molecules act when they become a gas?"

Carefully move students to the generalization that heat transforms solids into liquids and then into gases. The class enjoys watching the other students wiggle and fly around as they assume the role of molecules turning into a gas. The last part of the demonstration was the idea that, when an object is frozen, the molecules have stopped moving altogether. The demonstration and follow-up questions usually spark a lot of discussion and more questions.

Suggestions for Differentiating Instruction

Interest and student motivation are paramount in this activity. Challenge students to discover how molecules are everywhere. The students are part of a hands-on demonstration trying to answer their questions about molecules. Teachers modify instruction when they ask for volunteers to play the role of molecules even though they want all students to participate. Collaborative group work is encouraged; time for discussion and lots of communication take place in this differentiated hands-on activity.

Activity 4: Floating Objects (Grades 3–6)

Inquiry Skills

Hypothesizing, experimenting, and communicating.

Science Standards

Inquiry, physical science, science and technology, personal perspectives, and written communications.

Description

The weight of water gives it pressure. The deeper the water, the more pressure. Pressure is also involved when something floats. For an object to float, opposing balanced forces work against each other. Gravity pulls down on the object and the water pushes it up. The solution to floating is the object's size relevant to its weight. If it has a high volume and is light for its size, then it has a large surface area for the water to push against. In this activity, students will explore what objects will float in water. All students should try to float some of these objects.

Materials

large plastic bowl or aquarium	salt
bag of small objects to test	ruler
(paper clip, nail, block, key, etc.)	spoon
oil-base modeling clay	paper towels
large washers	kitchen foil, 6-inch square

Procedure

1. Have the students fill the plastic bowl half full with water.
2. Direct the students to empty the bag of objects onto the table along with the other items.
3. Next, have students separate the objects into two groups: the objects that will float and the objects that will sink. Encourage students to record their predictions in their science/math journal.
4. Have students experiment by trying to float all the objects and record what happened in their science/math journals.

Evaluation

Have students reflect on these thinking questions and respond in their math/science journals. Encourage students to work together helping students who are having trouble expressing their ideas.

1. What is alike about all the objects that floated? sank?
2. What can be done to sink the objects that floated?
3. What can be done to float the objects that sank?
4. In what ways can a piece of foil be made to float? sink?
5. Describe how a foil boat can be made.
6. How many washers will the foil boat carry?
7. What could float in salt water that cannot float in fresh water?
8. Encourage students to try to find something that will float in fresh water and sink in salt water.

Suggestions for Differentiating Instruction

Spell out the purpose of the activity. Students have fun experimenting with what will float. Students construct boats made from aluminum foil. This motivating activity looks at water pressure, gravity, volume, weight, and ways to solve problems. The teacher differentiates by making it clear what students are to learn. She understands, appreciates, and builds on student differences, adjusting content, process, and product in response to student readiness, interests, and learning profile.

Activity 5: Experimenting with Pennies (Grades 2–5)

Inquiry Skills

Hypothesizing, experimenting, and communicating.

Science Standards

Inquiry, earth science, science and technology, personal perspectives, and written communications.

Description

Students will determine how many drops of water will fit on a penny in an experiment that demonstrates water cohesion and surface tension.

Materials

- one penny for each pair of students
- glasses of water
- paper towels
- eye droppers (one for each pair of students)

Procedures

Have elementary students work with a partner. As a class, have them guess how many drops of water will fit on the penny. Record their guesses on the chalkboard. Ask students if it would make a difference if the penny was heads or tails. Also, record these guesses on the chalkboard. Instruct the students to try the experiment by using an eye dropper, a penny, and a glass of water. Encourage students to record their findings in their science journal. Bring the class together again. Encourage students to share their findings with the class.

Introduce the concept of cohesion. (Cohesion is the attraction of like molecules for each other. In solids and liquids, the force is strongest. It is cohesion that holds a solid or liquid together. There is also an attraction among water molecules for each other.) Introduce and discuss the idea of surface tension. (The molecules of water on the surface hold together so well that they often keep heavier objects from breaking through. The surface acts as if it is covered with skin.)

Evaluation, Completion, and/or Follow-up

Have students explain how this activity showed surface tension. Instruct students to draw what surface tension looked like in their science journal. What makes the water drop break on the surface of the penny? (It is gravity.) What other examples can students think of where water cohesion can be observed? (rain on a car windshield or window in a classroom, for example). Even disinterested students can relate to this activity if drawn into the conversation.

At the upper elementary and middle school levels, students can learn about the properties of substances. Hopefully, they understand that the atom is the smallest unit of matter that has mass and takes up space. All matter is made up of atoms, which are too small to see through a microscope. Also, atoms and molecules are always in motion (Keeley, Eberle, & Dorsey, 2008).

Suggestions for Differentiating Instruction

The teacher differentiates by modifying instruction based on her or his ongoing assessment of students' science knowledge. The teacher explains what students are to learn and gives them opportunities to work with a partner. Students observe, ask questions, discuss, and record their findings. Writing about surface tension is an important follow-up activity.

Activity 6: Forming a Static Electric Horse (Grades 3–6)

Inquiry Skills

Hypothesizing, experimenting, and communicating.

Science Standards

Inquiry, physical science, science and technology, personal perspectives, and written communications.

Objectives and Description

1. Students will have an opportunity to explore static electricity.
2. No previous knowledge of static electricity is necessary.
3. Students will learn more through fun, hands-on experimentation about the concepts of static electricity (positive and negative charges).

Materials

- 1 inflated balloon for each student
- scissors
- tag board horse patterns
- colored tissue paper
- crayons and/or markers

Procedures

1. Short introduction focusing on the horses and a mystery question: ask students if they think they could make a paper horse move without touching it? (no mention yet of static electricity concepts).
2. Teacher describes how to construct the horse:
   a. Fold the paper in half and trace the horse pattern on one side of tissue paper. (Trace forms are passed out.)
   b. Fold both halves of tissue paper together, cut out pattern—making sure to leave the horse joined together at the top of its head and tail.
   c. Decorate (color) both sides of the horse.
3. Teacher describes how to "electrify" the paper horse:
   a. Students place their horse on smooth surface.
   b. They rub a balloon over their hair a few times.
   c. Students hold the balloon in front of the horse.
4. The teacher passes out the balloons.
5. Next, the teacher instructs the students to get in groups of four or five sitting around the table.
6. Now, students "electrify" their horses and have short races across tables.
7. After the races have ended, have a class discussion on what happened between balloon and horse.

8. Ask students to describe their views. Then, add the scientific explanation describing static electricity: The outer layer of electrons from atoms on the hair is rubbed off and clings to the atoms of the balloon, producing static electricity. When students hold the positively charged balloon close to the uncharged (negatively charged) horse, there is a strong attraction between them—and the horse races toward the balloon.

Evaluation

1. Instruct students to write in their journals about their experiment.
2. Some possible assignments follow:
   - In their own words, have students explain the connections among the horse, the balloon, and static electricity. For students struggling to write about "their horse" or afraid to construct a horse for themselves, have them work with the small group and come up with a group statement of the experiment.
   - Have students write a short story about their horse in the race.
   - Illustrate the "electric" horse race; provide a commentary.
   - Have the group write an article for the school newspaper describing their experiment.

Post-assessment

Assessment is based on observing the students and from reading their written/illustrated journals about their experiments.

Suggestions for Differentiating Instruction

The teacher attends to student differences. In a differentiated classroom, the teacher is aware of individual differences. She uses a broad range of learning strategies such as writing. Writing and reflecting on their science experiences helps students make sense of their own ideas.

Activity 7: Observing the Rain Forest (Grades K–2)

Inquiry Skills

Hypothesizing, experimenting, and communicating.

Science Standards

Inquiry, life science, science and technology, personal perspectives, and written communications.

Description

This inclusive science activity is designed for all students, but it's an ideal lesson to use for Limited English Proficient (LEP) learners. It encourages the students to come together and establish themselves as groups. Speaking and writing are not mandatory! The only adaptation required in this activity is a simple color coding of the identifying cards that will enable the student to visualize what other students (plants and animals) he or she is connected with, rather than just reading the card.

Additional adaptations might include pictures of the plant or animal on the cards that show the actual relationship or more color coding by matching the color of the yarn to the color of the cards. The student will be able to see his or her group members by the colors, pictures, and yarns, and understand the interrelationships, without having to read the card.

This is a valuable lesson not only for LEP students but also for students with other language deficiencies and all students within the classroom. The exceptional student will not be singled out, and all the students can benefit by the simple color classification. The color coding and pictures serve to reinforce the written relationships, and the students will receive graphic, physical examples of the purpose of the activity to show interdependence. The activity will also help increase social interaction within the classroom and might help break down the barrier caused by the difference in language.

The evaluation and conclusion to this activity will be for students to discuss and then write their reaction to, or interpretation of, what occurred when the connections were broken. This will be an opportunity for the student and his or her classmates to artistically describe the lesson.

Rain Forest Interdependence

Objectives

1. Students will follow directions, participate in all activities, and work cooperatively with their classmates.
2. Students will discuss, as a class, their feelings about this activity.
3. Students will draw a picture of the interdependence of the rain forest.
4. Students will utilize some of the information that has been gained in the previous lessons.

Materials

Plant and animal cards pasted on 3 × 5 index cards
Pictures of rain forest plants and animals

Yarn (three-yard pieces) for three pieces per student
Paper and other art supplies

Preparation

1. Teachers, aides, or student helpers will cut and paste pictures of plant
   and animal cards onto 3 × 5 cards for each student.
2. Pictures or books of rain forest plants and animals should be available
   for reference, if needed.
3. Move the desks to the edges of the classroom so that the students can
   move around.

Procedures

1. Distribute one card to each student.
2. Pass out several long pieces of yarn to each student.
3. Each student will read their card and then find the person or people
   that are related to theirs.
4. When a match or relationship is made, the students then attach themselves with a long piece of yarn (tie around wrist). More than two
   students can be connected, for example, kapok tree will be attached
   to parrots, insects, and so forth.
5. If a student wants more information, direct them to the pictures and
   other reference material.

Evaluation

1. The class will discuss, while still connected, how it feels to depend on
   the other organisms?
2. Instruct students to guess in what part of the rain forest their plant or
   animal lives: canopy, understory, or forest floor?
3. Have students reflect on these questions:
   - What plant or animal did you represent?
   - What do you depend on for food or shelter?
   - How does it feel to have so many connections?
   - What did you learn from this activity?
   - Would you like to live in a rain forest? Why?
4. The teacher may then cut several pieces of the yarn that are attached to
   the kapok tree and ask the class the following questions:
   - What would happen if the kapok tree is cut down?
   - What other animals would be affected?
5. After discussing the effects of the destruction of a part of this delicate
   ecosystem, the students may come up with some other ideas.

Suggestions for Differentiating Instruction. Teachers can differentiate instruction by modifying instruction based on their knowledge of the topic. They implement the children's book *The Great Kapok Tree: A Tale of the Amazon Rain Forest* by Lynne Cherry (1990). This is a story of a young man chopping down a great kapok tree in the rain forest. He becomes tired and falls asleep. One by one, the animals who live around the tree emerge to beg him not to destroy their home.

As the teacher continues to read, students pay close attention to the animals hidden in the foliage. Ask children to predict what will happen next. There are a host of exciting possibilities for teaching young readers. Things to do after reading, art, drama, science, conservation, and environmental issues all come into play.

Activity 8: Experimenting with Ramps (Grades 6–9)

Inquiry Skills

Observation, prediction, measurement, and data recording.

Science Standards

Inquiry and physical science.

Description

Students will compare how objects go down inclined planes.

Objectives

Students will learn about the concept of balance. A balance is a way of physically comparing two objects or groups of objects. Students will develop and extend their understanding of balance as they construct and use ramps (slides) that convey the important concept of how balance works. They will compare how objects go down the ramps (slides). Students will learn about the concept of balance and how balance works.

Procedures

Form the class into groups of four.
Give each group a block and a ramp (paper towel roll cut lengthwise).
Show the group how to make a slide by taping a ramp to a block.

1. Have the students make slides, making sure they are identical (the slopes form the same angle). Then, have the group of students align

their slides along the edge of a table. Use a block to form a barrier at the other end of the table.
2. Set out the objects for students to test their slides (paper clips, balls, marbles, dice, cylinder-shaped blocks, paper towel rolls, penny, rocks, and masking tape rolls). Students will record their predictions of the objects that will reach the barrier and those that won't. Encourage students to record their predictions with a partner and state their reasons. Test all the objects.

Evaluation

Have students explain how this activity showed balance. Have students write their reflections. Discuss which objects reached the barrier and which did not. Have students describe and compare the distance each traveled.

Activity 9: Recyclable Materials Construction

Inquiry Skills

Observation, prediction, measurement, and data recording.

Science Standards

Science inquiry, physical science, science and technology, math and science, coordination, and problem solving.

Description

One of the exciting things that can happen during technological problem solving is that students develop and construct their own best solutions. This middle school activity moves beyond conducting experiments or finding solutions to word problems (all students doing the same task at the same time). In "hands-on technology," students are not shown a solution. Typically, this results in some very creative and innovative designs.

Using the tools and materials found in many classrooms or school technology laboratories, students design and construct solutions that allow them to apply the process skills. The products they create and engineer in the technology lab often use a wide range of materials such as plastics, woods, electrical supplies, and so on.

During the course of solving their problem, students are forced to test hypotheses and frequently generate new questions. This involves a lot of scientific investigation and mathematical problem solving, but it is quite different from the routine classroom tasks. In this activity, a problem is introduced to the class.

Working in small groups of four or five students, their challenge is to plan a way of coming up with a solution. Students are to document the steps they used along the way. Some suggestions: have students brainstorm and discuss with friends, draw pictures, show design ideas, use mathematics, present technical drawings, work together, and consult with experts.

Background Information

The best construction materials are strong, yet lightweight. Wood is unexpectedly strong for its weight and, therefore, well suited for many structures. Larger buildings often use steel reinforced concrete beams, rather than wood, in their construction. However, steel and concrete are both heavy, presenting problems in construction. A lighter material would be a great alternative and a best seller in the construction industry. This could be done by reinforcing the beam with a material other than steel—ideally, a recyclable material.

Problem

Design the lightest and strongest beam possible by reinforcing concrete with one or more recyclable materials: aluminum cans, plastic milk jugs, plastic soda bottles, and/or newspapers. Students must follow the construction constraints. The beam will be weighed. Then, it will be tested by supporting it at each end, and a load will be applied to the middle.

The load will be increased until the beam breaks. The load divided by the beam weight will give the load-to-weight ratio. The designer of the beam with the highest load-to-weight ratio will be awarded the contract.

Construction Limits

The solution must

1. be made into a reusable mold that the student designs;
2. result in a forty-centimeter-long (approximately sixteen inches) beam that fits within a volume of 1,050 cubic centimeters (approximately sixty-four cubic inches); and
3. be made from concrete and recyclable materials.

Objectives

1. Groups of students will plan and design their beam.
2. Groups will work on their construction plans.

3. Students will design and construct their beam.
4. Students will gather information from a variety of resources and make sketches of all the possibilities they considered.
5. Students will record the science, mathematics, and technology principles used.

Procedures

1. Divide students into small groups of three or four students.
2. Present the problem to the class.
3. Students will discuss and draw out plans for how to construct a beam. All students should be part of this process.
4. Students will design a concrete beam reinforced with recycled materials.
5. Students will work together to construct, measure, and test the beam.
6. Students will present their invention to the class.

Evaluation

Students will document their work in a portfolio that includes the following:

1. Sketches of all the possibilities their group considered
2. A graphic showing how their invention performed
3. Descriptions of the process skills used in their solution
4. Information and notes gathered from resources
5. Thoughts and reflections about this project

Some students may need assistance in their designs. Encourage them to work together on their construction.

DIFFERENTIATED INSTRUCTION: IMAGINATION AND TEAMWORK

In a differentiated classroom, the teacher attends to students' interests, learning styles, prior needs, and comfort zones. Frequent group activity sessions give students many opportunities to question data, design and conduct real experiments, and expand their thinking beyond the classroom experience. Learning is frequently done as a cohesive group in which individual student ideas and strengths are shared. Teamwork also supports learners as they gain the ability to think unconventionally, generate new scenarios, and produce imaginative work.

Teachers can use tiered activities so all students can focus on basic understandings and skills but at different levels of complexity. By keeping the focus of the activity the same, but offering ways of access at varying degrees of difficulty, the teacher gets the most out of each student so that each student comes away with essential skills and each student is appropriately challenged (Smutny & von Fremd, 2009). Another way to differentiate is to encourage different students or small groups to come up with unique products that more closely meet their interests, needs, and learning style(s).

SUGGESTIONS FOR TEACHERS NEW TO DIFFERENTIATED INSTRUCTION

Many teachers like the concept of differentiated instruction, but some aren't quite sure how to get started. Here are a few suggestions:

1. *Assess students.*

   The role of assessment is to foster worthwhile learning for all students. Sometimes, assessment is as simple as an informal teacher observation of students at work. Performance assessments, portfolios, and informal assessment tools such as rubrics, checklists, and anecdotal records are helpful. Teachers may use a compacting strategy. This strategy encourages teachers to assess students before beginning a unit of study or development of a skill. Formative assessment during a lesson helps.

2. *Create complex instruction tasks.*

   Complex tasks are
   - open-ended,
   - intrinsically interesting to students,
   - uncertain (thus allowing for a variety of solutions),
   - involve real objects, and
   - draw upon multiple intelligences in a real-world way.

3. *Use television in the classroom.*

   Television's wide accessibility has the potential for making learning available for students who do not perform well in traditional classroom situations. It can reach students on their home ground, but the most promising place is in the classroom.

4. *Use materials and activities that address a wide range of reading levels, learning profiles, and student interests.*

   Include activities that range from simple to complex, from concrete to abstract.

5. *Use science notebooks.*

   Science notebooks are an everyday part of learning. The science notebook is more than a record of collected data and facts of what students have learned. They are notebooks of students' questions, predictions, claims linked to evidence, conclusions, and reflections. A science notebook is a central place where language, data, and experiences work together to produce meaning for the students.

Notebooks support differentiated learning. They are helpful when addressing the needs of disinterested students. In a science notebook, even students who may have poor writing skills can use visuals such as drawings, graphs, and charts to indicate their learning preferences. There is ongoing interaction in the notebooks. For teachers, a notebook provides a window into students' thinking and offers support for all students.

6. *Provide clear directions for students.*

Teachers need to offer instructions about what a student could do if he or she needs help.

7. *Use a record-keeping system to monitor what students do.*

8. *Include a plan for ongoing assessment.*

Teachers use ongoing assessment of student readiness, interest, and learning profile for the purpose of matching tasks to students' needs. Some students struggle with many things; others are more advanced, but most have areas of strengths. Teachers do not assume that one set of skills fits all students.

9. *Modify a curricular element (content, process, and products).*

There are times when changes have to be made so that students will understand important ideas and skills more thoroughly. Remember, it is always best to provide a cultural mindset of raising expectations that are built on the assumption that all students can be successful if given the right opportunities.

SCIENTIFIC INQUIRY AND ITS ASSOCIATES

Science is a process of describing nature and creating theoretical systems to explain natural phenomena. Uncovering the secrets of nature is a prime motivator in scientific inquiry. The main activity of scientists is learning about the nature of things through observation. In addition, they create hypotheses, test them, and draw conclusions. At any level, science involves reasoning, inquiry, and discovery. Thinking skills, mathematics, and technology are key ingredients because they are essential to the accurate description and explanation of events in nature.

Science also teaches values like respect for evidence, openness, accountability, and tolerance for opposing points of view. When it comes to the technological products of science, it isn't just about computers. It's about students becoming critical thinkers, innovators, and learners of a wide range of technology tools.

In the classroom, a good way to get science inquiry started is through authentic questions generated from student experiences. The next step is the exploration of ideas, experimentation, and the use of creative and innovative thinking skills.

Asking questions, observations, reading, planning, conducting investigations, experimenting, providing explanations, and communicating the results are all part of the inquiry package. In addition, posing new questions, generating curiosity, and developing observation skills are all found along the road to enable students to actively seek their own answers. Imaginative written, oral, and group communication skills all matter.

Students develop effective interpersonal skills as they work together, pose questions, and critically examine data. Successful science lessons are often organized around real-life problems in a way that can elicit thoughtful behavior and shared decision making. This often involves designing and conducting real experiments that carry thoughtful behavior beyond the classroom.

More attention is given to science-related issues that have an impact on responsible citizenship and self-understanding. Goals include using scientific knowledge to make wise decisions and solve difficult problems related to life and living. As you might imagine, twenty-first-century science cannot be isolated from human welfare and social-economic progress—it has dimensions that extend into ethics, values, law, and the social sciences.

Science is not only becoming more interdisciplinary; it is reaching directly into new domains. For example, some of the science research fields that are emerging are biochemistry, biophysics, plant engineering, terrestrial biology, and neurobiology. The elementary and middle school curriculum is beginning to reflect these new realities.

As far as inquiry is concerned, it is not all that new to include reasoning, problem solving, and innovative thinking in lessons for *some* students. What *is* new is including them in lessons for *all* students. There is general agreement among science educators today that all individuals, not just an elite, should have the opportunity to become creative and innovative thinkers.

Learning about science involves more than becoming familiar with today's scientific issues and the key concepts that underlie them. To understand and use science also requires an awareness of how science uses mathematical and technological tools to affect our culture, our lives, and our future.

SUMMARY, CONCLUSION, AND A PATH TO THE FUTURE

Efforts to improve science instruction stem from the national recognition of the importance of science and a scientifically literate citizenry. As far as the teacher is concerned, the NSE Standards suggest instructing students in a way that helps them engage in inquiry and make good use of scientific knowledge. This includes connecting the implications of science to their personal lives and to society. The majority of American schools have made changes based on the science standards. And these guidelines have influenced the design of everything from science textbooks to state science curriculum frameworks.

Inquiry is the basis for all science; it is used by everyone from practicing scientists to elementary school students. It starts with observation and then applies what is learned through observation to problem solving.

The standards point to inquiry learning as the way to connect what occurs in the world of science to active collaborative learning in the classroom. Inquiry-based instruction (inquiry teaching) is also viewed as the way to bring science to all students. Instead of mostly "chalk-and-talk," the teacher asks far more questions than they can answer. Also, the teacher is more of an organizer and facilitator; students share in learning responsibilities.

In a differentiated classroom, students are encouraged to collaborate and share responsibility for learning and work. Instruction focuses on important goals and standards in a way that helps students build a meaningful and accurate knowledge base. Student readiness, interests, needs, and learning preferences are all considered in lesson planning. Meaning and understanding may be viewed as originating from scientific inquiry in a way that helps students work together to develop creative and innovative powers of mind.

Differentiated science instruction also recognizes how important mathematics and technology are to developing the skills needed to become scientifically literate. Another part of the instructional package is making sure that students learn how to apply the appropriate scientific principles, processes, and technological tools.

It has been estimated that nearly 80 percent of the jobs in the near future will be cerebral and about 20 percent, manual. (Sixty years ago, the ratio was just the opposite.) This doesn't mean that every student now has to go to university, but everyone *does* need a high-quality *education* that provides them with good technical, problem-solving, and communications skills.

Learning how to learn is yet another skill that every student in every classroom will need for the world in which they will live. Being able to think outside of the lines is bound to be part of the package. Another skill that will be part of any conceivable future is having the ability to go beyond following instructions to figuring out how to change them.

When scientific understanding is coupled with the ability of the human imagination to invent new technologies, it may be possible to come up with everything from carbon-eating trees to nanotechnology that can go into the bloodstream and do repairs. Whether it's in the science lab or in the classroom, fresh approaches and ideas are more possible and more desirable than ever.

As scientifically knowledgeable teachers build up their pedagogical competency, informal ideas, and judgments, they will be increasingly able to invent the science classrooms of the future. But what about predicting the science-related parts of the future?

The pieces of the math, science, and technology puzzle are constantly changing shape, so how they might come together is a mystery. Still, one useful thing that can come from thinking about the future is raising hopes about our ability to positively influence the direction. Another plus is learning to turn ambiguity in a positive direction.

But the truths of science and the advances of technology are so well concealed and unpredictable that the only thing we can be sure of is that much of what we believe is going to happen won't. As economist John Kenneth Galbraith said, "The only function of forecasting the future is to make astrology look respectable."[4]

REFERENCES

Keeley, P., Eberle, F., & Dorsey, C. (2008). *Uncovering student ideas in science: Another 25 formative assessment probes.* Arlington, VA: National Science Teachers Association (NSTA) Press.

Krajcik, J., & Czerniak, C. (2007). *Teaching science in elementary and middle school: A project-based approach* (3rd ed.). New York: Lawrence Erlbaum Associates.

National Research Council (NRC). (2000). *Inquiry and the national science education standards.* Washington, DC: National Academy Press.

Renzulli, J., & Reis, S. (2008). *Enriching curriculum for all students* (2nd ed.). Thousand Oaks, CA: Corwin Press.

Saracho, O., & Spodek, B. (2008). *Contemporary perspectives on science and technology in early childhood education.* Charlotte, NC: Information Age Publishing (IAP).

Slotta, J., & Linn, M. (2009). *WISE science: Web-based inquiry in the classroom.* New York: Teachers College Press. (WISE stands for Web-Based Inquiry Science Environment.)

Smutny, J., & von Fremd, S. (2009). *Igniting creativity in gifted learners, K–6: Strategies for every teacher.* Thousand Oaks, CA: Corwin Press.

Tomlinson, C., Brimijoin, K., & Narvaez, L. (2008). *The differentiated school: Making revolutionary changes in teaching and learning.* Alexandria, VA: ASCD.

Victor, E., Kellough, R., & Tai, R. (2008). *Science K–8: An integrated approach* (11th ed.). Upper Saddle River, NJ: Pearson Prentice Hall.

RESOURCES AND SUGGESTED READINGS

Adams, D., & Hamm, M. (2000). *Literacy today: New standards across the curriculum.* New York: Falmer Press/Routledge.

American Association for the Advancement of Science. (2001). *Atlas of science literacy*. Washington, DC: American Association for the Advancement of Science.

Burke, K. (2010). *How to assess authentic learning*. Thousand Oaks, CA: Corwin Press.

Costa, A., & Kallick, B. (2008). *Learning and leading with habits of the mind: 16 essential characteristics for success*. Alexandria, VA: Association for Supervision and Curriculum Development.

Dewey, J. (1933). *How we think*. Boston: Houghton Mifflin.

Freely, J. (2009). *Aladdin's lamp: How Greek science came to Europe through the Islamic world*. New York: Alfred A. Knopf.

Gredier, M., & Shields, C. (2008). *Vygotsky's legacy: A foundation for research and practice*. New York: Guilford Press.

Miller, E., & Almon, J. (2009). Crisis in kindergarten: Why children need to play in school. Available at www.allianceforchildhood.org/.

Sousa, D. (2008). *How the brain learns mathematics*. Thousand Oaks, CA: Corwin Press.

Tapscott, D. (2008). *Grown up digital: How the net generation is changing your world*. New York: McGraw-Hill.

Tomlinson, C., et al. (2009). *The parallel curriculum: A design to develop learner potential and challenge advanced learners*. Thousand Oaks, CA: Corwin Press.

Zoeliner, T. (2009). *Uranium: War, energy, and the rock that shaped the world*. New York: Viking.

5

Technology and Education

Creativity, Innovation, and Preparing for the Future

All of our inventions are . . . but improved means to an unimproved end.

—Henry David Thoreau[1]

Technology is an increasingly powerful and unpredictable force for change in the twenty-first century. In addition, the way we consume media has changed and will continue to change. So, it is little wonder that understanding the implications of a world filled with the technological by-products of mathematics and science is coming to be viewed as a necessity for everyone. Fortunately, you don't have to be an information technology (IT) expert to have enough of a grasp of what's going on to intelligently discuss the important issues.

This chapter presents teachers with some ideas and techniques that will help them adapt quickly and do a better job of using high-tech tools to differentiate instruction. The basic idea is to make technology-related lessons more compelling in a way that can reach the different needs and learning styles of all students. Encouraging creative and innovative thoughtfulness is a central theme. Topics include the impact of standards and connecting students to a technology-intensive world. We also explore the following:

- How differentiating technology instruction changes learning
- Understanding and taking control of multiple media symbol systems
- Evaluating multimedia software and Internet access to the world of ideas
- The promise, pitfalls, and social effects of converging technologies

It is hoped that by offering suggestions on the productive use of digital technologies, light is shed on some of the technological implications for the mathematics and science standards. Along the innovative *and* practical way, suggestions are made for integrating computers, calculators, video, and the Internet into daily lessons.

In tomorrow's classrooms, the intelligent use of digital tools will play a key role in helping students ask the right questions, create new ideas, and successfully deal with the unstable frontiers of the twenty-first century. Of course, it's hard to come up with answers when nobody even knows what the questions will be. Still, chaos and uncertainty frequently open up opportunities for developing new ideas and new patterns of behavior. In uncertain times, resistance to change is lower so that shifts are more likely to occur and inspiration is more likely to happen. And historically, many of the greatest insights and innovations have shown up during unstable times.

Randomness and uncertainty may rule, however, in any conceivable future; innovative thinking, resiliency, and a strong immune system are bound to help. Also, you can be sure that *learning to think* and *thinking to learn* will be partners in student achievement.

In teaching for creative, critical, and innovative thinking, it's important to figure out what students already know. And it's equally important to know what to do when students don't know something.

As far as encouraging students to generate imaginative new ideas, it is important that *everyone* have the chance to engage in higher-level thinking, collaborative inquiry, problem solving, and meaningful communication. Innovative approaches to problems or situations require a deep understanding of resources available today before it becomes possible to invent beyond them. Also, time, vision, teamwork, and resources play important roles in innovation.

Necessity is often a motivating factor as well. In addition, successful innovation frequently involves discarding assumptions, building on the ideas of others, and tapping into networks. A note of caution here: new ideas frequently disturb the status quo, and instant results are hard to come by (Evans, 2004).

It may be challenging, but you can be sure that countries that figure out ways to make their populations smarter, more technologically savvy, and increasingly innovative are the ones that will thrive down the road.

TECH MAGIC, MYTHS, NETWORKING, AND THE CREATIVE IMAGINATION

Providing new capacities for thinking and learning digital technologies is dramatically changing the face of instruction and the nature of childhood itself. The same high-tech tools have also proved to be helpful in making subject matter more engaging and relevant for all students. In one form or another, technology has long been an intrinsic part of cultural and educational systems. But when computers came along, they amplified the influence and educators realized that these tools had to be part of any effort to improve instruction or redesign schools.

As we move toward the future, all media seem to be digital. Still, like just about anything else in the classroom, success depends on teachers who are prepared to provide their students with the advantages that technology can bring. It is always good to inject a little healthy skepticism into the debate, by paying attention to the myths, as well as the magic of innovation and technology.

For an example, do you think that countries where the schools pay more attention to rote learning can't innovate? As Bill Gates said, "I have never met the guy who doesn't know how to multiply who created software . . ."[2] He has also pointed out that some of Microsoft's most creative software engineers started their schooling in countries that made sure basic math, science, and technology skills were in place. A very different point of technological skepticism is made clear by the title of Mark Bauerlein's 2008 book: *The Dumbest Generation: How the Digital Age Stupefies Young Americans and Jeopardizes Our Future.*

Whether it is through chat rooms, Web threads, or face-to-face contacts, you can get a good discussion going about whether or not the Internet sites like Facebook, MySpace, and Twitter can empower group fixations that shut out the voices of adults, history, current events, and so forth. Are there ways to make the constant babble of thoughts useful—or is the whole thing the antithesis of intellectual discourse?

By the way, the Nielsen Online rating system reports that Twitter is losing users at a much quicker pace than other popular online hangouts like Facebook or MySpace did at comparable stages of their development. Tweets stop at 140 characters, often summing up descriptions of trivial events like eating or drinking. Still, either a brief memo or tweeted photo can have impact.

Twitter is so decentralized that it is difficult for a government or other censoring agencies to control. Unlike other social networking sites, when you tweet on Twitter you don't need a browser or Internet access; you can go directly from phone to phone. Another difference is the ease with which it accommodates the social needs of the general public, rather than just a circle of "friends" in your network.

Twitter's interactivity also makes it easy for an anonymous text messenger to insert words and terms into the text. This underlines the fact that anyone with low-budget digital technology, like a text-capable cell phone, can influence real-world events and take part in creating a virtual collective stream of consciousness.

Might networking technologies, with their spirit of perpetual accelera-
tion, have the potential of turning political life into a frenzy, cheapening
the language, or diminishing the kind of creative greatness that isn't available on Facebook or Twitter feeds?

PAYING ATTENTION TO
THE ESSENTIALS OF LEARNING

Even if social networking sites are off limits at school, it is important to
deal with the issues surrounding them. Young people, for example, need
to know about posting personal things online, including being aware of
dangers ranging from loss of privacy to predatory behavior.

Ask students if they want their parents, friends, or teachers to see what
they post; sooner or later, some of them will. Remember, if something is
online, it doesn't go away and it's easy for anyone to get access to it. A chat
room, for example, is only as private as every member wants it to be. Using
the Internet for personal connections is a little like crossing the street—you
have to carefully look both ways first.

From the invention of the printing press to the telegraph, to radio and
television, to computers and the Internet, innovation has always generated
both good and bad possibilities. Although the global promise of digital
technology like the Internet is limitless, governments can manipulate it and
extremist groups can exploit it.

But whether the use is bad, good, or in between, technologies from websites to cell phones and text messaging can make a real difference on many
levels. But technology will never deliver us from either ignorance or evil.
Only good people with an understanding of both the media and the message can do that. As far as useful educational opportunities are concerned,
digital technology opens up useful possibilities for all students. Positive
examples include scientific simulation, virtual field trips, and interactive
political action through social networking.

Although the essentials of learning matter more than novelties of new
media, the complete avoidance of digital technology is not an option. There
is, after all, general agreement that the key to a nation's economic success
lies in having an educational system that can produce students who know
about technological tools and work well in collaborative contexts that are
creative, innovative, and flexible (Yelland, 2007). This means that everybody needs at least enough post–high school training to be competent in
fields that require technical expertise.

Computers and their attendant technologies at least have the possibility
of evolving in ways that help students acquire the ability to reason, empa-
thize, and come up with new ideas. Digital tools can also open up possi-

bilities for more active and differentiated engagement with subject matter. Regardless of their age, students learn fundamental concepts more successfully (and are more able to apply them) through interactive, collaborative, student-centered learning (Hamilton, 2007). Digital technology can help by allowing collaboration with peers at home and around the world.

Can the creative imagination invent technologies that can solve just about any problem? The brief history of digital technology is filled with people who made confident predictions about the best routes to the future, believed their predictions, and had trouble when things didn't work out quite the way they thought they would.

Examples include the paperless office, the Y2K millennium bug, and the idea that online courses would completely take the place of face-to-face classes in actual universities. Still, technological innovation requires approaching the future by thinking broadly and being bold. It also requires appreciating the strategies for innovation that worked in the past—while adapting to rapidly changing realities.

THINKING, LEARNING, AND THE
REACH OF TECHNOLOGY

When hearing the word "technology," polls show that two-thirds of the public think only of computers and the Internet. Only a third thought of technology as the process by which humans modify nature to meet their needs and wants (Rose & Dugger, 2003).

As far as the schools are concerned, technology is more than artifacts like computers and spacecraft; the knowledge and processes used to create and operate technological products are an important part of technology education. Also technology is more than the application of math and science. It may be built on, complement, and support these subjects, but it has a wider reach.

Definitions of technology education and educational technology vary, and concepts frequently overlap, but there is general agreement that learning with (or about) technology is much more than computers. It involves exploring the technological knowledge and skills used in the designed world—transportation, medical, transportation technology, and so forth.

Technology education also deals with the design processes and technological abilities that are applied to a wider range of human needs. Educational technology is a slightly different subject; it may be viewed as using technologies in the education of students: computer programs, the Internet, calculators, and even things like heat probes in science.

Since backgrounds and interests vary greatly, students need to approach technology in different ways to appreciate and understand the subject.

This requires classroom practice that allows for the differences in student interests, prior knowledge, socialization needs, and learning styles. In the differentiated classroom, teachers take care to vary the degree of structure in a lesson—as well as the pacing, complexity, and level of technical abstraction. The basic idea is that learning is most effective when adjustments are made so that a learner at any achievement level can make sense (meaning) out of whatever is being taught (Strickland, 2009).

Where technologies and their associates are taking us remains a mystery. At least a few of the consequences can be predicted. Many cannot. For example, who at the beginning of the twentieth century would have predicted the human consequences of physics and the technologies associated with atomic energy.

In another fifty years, the same thing may be said about posthuman evolution if machine intelligence reaches a stage where it can play a major role in the process of technological innovation. Why not encourage students to whimsically gaze into the beyond? They just might get a little of it right. Just make sure they're flexible and resilient enough to deal with the surprises.

Part of the excitement over what is just beyond the horizon is not knowing when the boundaries of effectiveness will shift and where things will end up. One example of a surprise that awaits us is associated with learning about the architecture of information storage in the human mind. Could self-aware digital systems eventually emerge from the interconnections of computers and computer networks?

From problem solving in mathematics to understanding the natural world (science), technological designs and tools have constraints that limit our choices. Still, the twenty-first century is a time to look out for all the new things that might show up on the horizon.

TECHNOLOGY, STANDARDS, AND SOCIAL VALUES

The math standards and the science standards make it clear that both high tech (computers) and low tech (simple manipulatives) are essential to problem solving and inquiry. The technology standards focus on the digital side of the equation. All of the standards suggest ways for technology to improve instruction for all students.

A major point is that every student should have access to high-quality content so common learning goals can be reached. In math and science, for example, the underlying assumption is that students should not be limited to executing basic rules and remembering fundamental concepts. Aiming low and slow just doesn't get the job done. When in doubt, it is best to "teach up" with strategies that engage the imagination with the help of active learning and group participation (Gregory & Chapman, 2006).

As English writer and thinker G. K. Chesterton once remarked, "Education is the soul of a society as it passes from one generation to another."[3] Education, like technology, both shapes *and* reflects the values found in society. Take the example of digital technology: learners can be isolated *or* encouraged to join with others. Those who think that it is all good or all bad miss the point.

In our personal and civic lives, technology can slip through our hands to limit our choices at work and erode the edges of the constitutional rights of privacy in our daily lives. It can bring out the worst in human nature and diminish the imagination. On the other hand, technology can empower individuals, encourage students' curiosity, and spark innovation.

"We've heard a lot about how Google is making us dumber and more distracted and lazier," writes Scott Brown (2009) in *Wired* magazine. "We've heard less about how it's making us—maybe even forcing us to be—funnier." He goes on to suggest that, in the "digital hive mind" where comedy is colloquy, everything is "material" and life is "one big writer's room with witty one-upsmanship on blogs, social networking sites, in tweets, in funny video shorts, Locats and talk-backs." Brown's overall implication is that everyone must learn to be funny "because funny is becoming a language unto itself, the lingua franca of the wired world."

Of course, the shorthand approach of standup jokes may work well as comedy online. But unfortunately (or fortunately) in school, learning, and life it usually takes a lot more than a short punch line.

By the way, a "Locat" is a digital image (usually on the Internet) combining a photograph, often a cat, with a humorous caption. This can be made into a good activity, although we like to avoid the cats, dialects, and the broken English. Try the following activity:

- Find some pictures that have something to do with what students are studying; have pairs of students come up with a humorous caption or two that they can share with the whole class.
- Provide each student pair with some captions and have them draw the cartoons.

Again, they should share at least one with the whole class. If your equipment doesn't let you project a computer image onto a large screen in class, simply have students draw and write things out on an overhead transparency and project that. No overhead projector? Put it on a large piece of construction paper and make sure the result can be seen from twenty feet away.

Online and printed newspapers and other sources have plenty of single-frame cartoons (often with political or social commentary). Just take the caption off and let students come up with their own; or keep the caption and have them draw the cartoon. In spite of laugh lines, misplaced enthusiasm, and nuisances, technology is both a concern in its own right and an essential part of the math and science curriculum.

Like all technology through the ages, digital technology is a double-edged sword. At their out-of-school worst, games are rigidly preprogrammed arcadelike shoot-em-ups where children frantically click on icons for instant gratification. At their worst, computers and the Internet can turn mathematics, science, technology, or any other topic into a spectator sport. Instead of an hour of chalk-and-talk, it's an hour of PowerPoint-and-talk.

At their in-school best, technology can be an excellent vehicle for individual and small group questioning, investigating, analyzing, communicating, and simulating content-related situations. Technological tools provide all kinds of possibilities for students to take control, solve problems, inquire collaboratively, and observe phenomena that would otherwise remain unobservable.

MATH, SCIENCE, AND TECHNOLOGY STANDARDS

The math, science, and technology standards all view technology as a means to form connections between natural and man-made worlds. There is also general agreement that it is important to pay attention to technological design and how technology can help students understand the big ideas of what is being studied. The standards also suggest that, in the elementary grades, students should be given opportunities to use all kinds of low-tech and high-tech technology to explore and design solutions to problems.

A suggested theme that reaches across subjects is helping students see the human factor and its societal implications. The laws of the physical and biological universe are viewed as important to understanding how technological objects and systems work. The standards also point to the importance of connecting students to the various elements of our technologically intensive world so they can construct models and imaginatively solve problems.

Many teachers are familiar with the math and science standards, but fewer know about the standards that relate directly to information and communication technology. The International Technology Education Association's *Standards for Technological Literacy* suggest that, within a sound educational setting, digital technology can enable students to become

- capable information technology users;
- information seekers, analyzers, and evaluators;
- problem solvers and decision makers;
- creative and effective users of productivity tools;

- communicators, collaborators, publishers, and producers; and
- informed, responsible, and contributing citizens (ITEA, 2000).

An essential skill set in the twenty-first century is the ability to understand and work with technology. This doesn't mean electronic worksheets because they are just as boring as the paper variety. So, it's important to make sure our digital tools take us someplace more interesting. The research suggests that frequent and intelligent use of some digital devices can help students achieve important technological capabilities (Adams, 2001).

Along the way, it helps if learners can develop the ability to sort through and evaluate the glut of information in cyberspace. It is also important to learn how to use data from search results (Google) to question, inquire, and solve problems. Like most things at school, making all these computer-related things happen has a lot to do with the capabilities of the classroom teacher. (See the International Society for Technology in Education's (ISTE) NETS*T project.)

TECHNOLOGY AND THE MATHEMATICS STANDARDS

The National Council of Teachers of Mathematics (NCTM) Standards include the use of technology in their core suggestions about how to teach mathematics. This is not all new; calculators have long been part of most mathematics programs.

Calculators are recommended for school mathematics programs to help develop number sense; skills in problem solving, mental computation, and estimation; and ability to see patterns, perform operations, and use graphics.

Calculators and other forms of technology continue to be used extensively in the home and office.

The cost of calculators and other forms of technology continues to decrease, while their power and functions continue to increase. Curriculum documents increasingly encourage the use of calculators and other forms of technology. Some tests currently available allow and even encourage calculator use (Cathcart, Pothier, Vance, & Bezuk, 2006).

EXPLORING MATH ACTIVITIES
USING CALCULATORS (GRADES 2–6)

You may not be able to afford a computer for every two students. But for a tiny fraction of that cost, you can still get some interesting points across with cheap calculators. The new mathematics recommendations specify that calculators should be continually made available for all students for use in activities like homework, class assignments, and tests. The following activities are just some suggestions for how to use calculators and computers in your classes. (These are examples of design activities that meet the math/science/technology standards: Standards 1, 2, 3, 4, 5, and 6.)

1. Use the Calculator to Improve Addition and Subtraction Estimation Skills (Grades 2–6)

Select two teams of students. Provide a calculator for each student. As the play begins, one member from the first team says a three-digit number. A player from team 2 says another three-digit number. Both players silently write an estimate of the sum of the two numbers. Players are limited to a five-second time limit to make estimates. Then, both players use the calculator to determine the sum. The player whose estimate is closest to the actual sum scores a point for the team. In case of a tie, both teams earn a point. The next player on each team assumes the same role.

The rules for subtraction are similar. One player from each team names a three-digit number. Both players then write down their estimates of the difference between the two numbers. Again, the player whose estimate is closest to the actual difference earns a point for the team. Students who engage in this activity for a while develop estimation strategies that benefit them in and out of the classroom.

2. Explore Calculator Patterns (Grades 2–6)

You need a calculator. Choose a number from 2 to 12. Press the "+" key. Press the "=" key. (You should see the number you first entered.) Keep pressing the "=" key. Each time you press, list the number displayed. Continue until there are at least twelve numbers on your list. Write down the patterns you notice (Burns, 2007).

3. Use Calculator Multiplication Puzzlers (Grades 4–9)

You need a calculator. For each problem, find the missing number by using the calculator and the problem-solving strategies of guessing and checking. Don't solve the problems by dividing; instead, see how many guesses you make for each problem. Record all of your guesses, for example

4 × ___ = 87

You might start with 23 and then adjust. Below is a possible solution that shows you how to record.

4 × 23 = 92
4 × 22 = 88

$4 \times 21 = 84$
$4 \times 21.5 = 86$
$4 \times 21.6 = 86.4$
$4 \times 21.7 = 86.8$
$4 \times 21.8 = 87.2$
$4 \times 21.74 = 86.96$
$4 \times 21.75 = 87$

4. Solve Problems with the Calculator: How Many Seconds Old Are You? (Grades 3–9)

Students may need to become familiar with the directions—how many seconds in a minute, a day, a month, a year? It's good to define the parameters. How old will you be at noon today? Encourage students to take a guess. Write it down. Use a calculator to find out. The problem requires several phases to its solution:

1. Decide what information is needed and where to collect it.
2. Choose the numerical information to use.
3. Do the necessary calculations.
4. Use judgment to interpret the results and make decisions about a possible solution.

5. Count with a Calculator (Grades 1–3)

The calculator can be used as a powerful counting tool. Important concepts of sequencing, placing value, and indicating one-to-one correspondence are learned through a child's physical interaction with this almost magical counting device.

To make a calculator count, enter the number 1 and press the "+" sign. Press the "+" sign again. Next press the "=" sign. Continue to press "=". The calculator will begin counting. Each time the "=" sign is pressed, the next number in sequence appears on the screen. If this set of instructions doesn't work with your calculator, check the specific device's directions. The directions should indicate how to get a constant function. Follow the directions on how to get a constant, and any of the counting activities will work for you (Reys, Suydam, & Lindquist, 2004).

6. Count Backward with a Calculator (Grades 1–3)

A calculator can also be programmed to count backward. Start with the number 1. Next, push the "-" sign. Push the "-" sign again, and then the number you want to count backward from appears. For example, if you wanted to count backward from 100, enter 1 - - 100 ===. When you press

"=", the calculator should show 99. Continue to press "=". With each press of the "=" button, the next number in reverse sequence appears. This is a great way to introduce children to counting backward.

7. Skip Counting with a Calculator (Grades 2–5)

A calculator can skip count also. Encourage students to count by 100s and 1,000s. Or, try skip counting by 3s, 5s, 7s, 9s, or whatever. You can begin counting with any number and skip count by any number. Have students try these calculator counting exercises, then make up their own. Encourage speculation about what the next number will be. Can you find a pattern?

$$5 + + 10 = = = =$$
$$3 + + 5 = = =$$
$$1{,}000 - 100 = = =$$

Try having a counting race. How long does it take counting by 1s to count to 1,000? How long would it take counting by 100s to count to 1,000,000?

USING TECHNOLOGY TO INVESTIGATE MATHEMATICS

The widespread impact of technology on nearly every aspect of our lives requires changes in the content and nature of school mathematics programs. The math standards suggest, in keeping with these changes, that students should be able to use calculators and computers to investigate mathematical concepts and increase their mathematical understanding.

Computers can be used to teach programming and data manipulation and to encourage drill and practice. Computer software is also used to present simulations, problem-solving materials, tutorials, and spatial visualizations. Many fine software programs provide a variety of problem-solving experiences. Some, such as What Do You Do with a Broken Calculator? involve computation. Others, such as The Factory and The Super Factory address spatial visualization. Still others, such as Math Shop, provide direct experiences with problem solving.

Other spreadsheet software like Geometer's Sketchpad is often underutilized in elementary and middle school. Sketchpad is a dynamic construction and exploration tool that enables students to explore and understand mathematics in ways that are simply not possible with traditional tools—or with other math software programs. With a scope that spans the mathematics curriculum from middle school to college, The Geometer's Sketchpad brings a powerful dimension to the study of mathematics.

With Sketchpad, students can construct an object and then explore its mathematical properties by dragging the object with the mouse. All mathematical relationships are preserved, allowing students to examine an entire set of similar cases in a matter of seconds and leading them to form generalizations. Sketchpad encourages a process of discovery in which students first visualize and analyze a problem and then make conjectures before attempting a proof. For system requirements, Sketchpad fully supports Windows and Macintosh on the same CD-ROM.

EMERGING TECHNOLOGIES AND IMAGINATION IN THE SCIENCE CLASSROOM

Science is more than discovery, making things, and technological inventiveness. Scientists aren't successful without a tremendous amount of creative and innovative reasoning because it's often not even clear what questions to ask—to say nothing of how pieces of an answer might come together.

Great scientists, like Galileo and Darwin, didn't introduce something into the world that was predetermined; they came up with imaginative and controversial new ideas that shaped the way we view the world. Adaptations, parodies, and borrowing have long been part of the creative process. Advances in technology follow a similar path.

The idea that science is composed of a catalog of facts that are not contested is false. Scientists know there are no final answers, and they usually acknowledge fallibility. The basic idea is to persuade, not compel. Science relies on the power of reason as new ideas are presented and tested in a rigorous process of peer review.

Even established scientific "truths" are subject to change when new evidence and concepts come into play. In spite of the search for objective facts, we must all deal with the fact that, for all their amazing power, math, science, and technology are profoundly human. Also, we must realize that, when knowledge is created, it can open up a Pandora's box of good and bad possibilities.

If schools are going to be transformed, educators need to understand the innovative possibilities associated with the technological products of science. In addition, new skills are required for new media. Cell phones are but one example of the good and bad things that come along with digital devices. They can bring a great class to a screeching halt—or they can be used to gather information and view scientists at work. Cell phones used to be hardware driven, but now software and networking possibilities are moving in to control the scene.

Yes, an array of digital technologies is today's growth segment, but don't bet on any one of them to dominate the scene. The dividing lines between smartphones, computers, television, and the Internet continue to blur.

With the recent improvements in wireless technologies, schools are doing more experimenting with all kinds of digital tools. Sometimes it works out, and sometimes it doesn't; a lot depends on knowledgeable teachers and the specific device that students are trying to use.

But no matter what technology is used, educators now realize that online and offline learning sometimes require different skills. Work on or off the Internet can be done collaboratively. But one of the differences with more traditional lessons is that the Internet amplifies the need for students to be able to sift through multiple sources of information and figure out what sources are valid and useful.

Clearly, dealing with a rapidly changing digital world requires new approaches and ideas. But how these new ideas get applied matters even more. How could the creativity and innovation success rates be doubled? Fail more often.

Although our focus is more on the digital side of the equation, technology is more than computers. Technological tools that are common to mathematics and science include the graphing calculator, motion detectors, and scientific probes that should be included in the teacher's repertoire. Graphing calculators and calculator-based lab (CBL) probes capture real data and generate a scatter plot of data. Good exploratory questions can be asked to generate more interesting functional relationships. You could, for example, ask students to create a linear descending line, a linear ascending line, a parabola, a horizontal line, and a vertical line using a motion detector. They will find this challenging, perhaps even impossible. But using probes and calculators allows students to look for patterns and to generalize many realistic formulas resulting from the graph of the data. The graphing calculator's statistical options allow for a formula or function relationship to emerge (Cathcart, Pothier, Vance, & Bezuk, 2006).

Although some of the lessons that follow can be accomplished without the use of technology, it can enrich the learning experience.

ACTIVITIES TO MOTIVATE SCIENCE LEARNERS

Activity Title: The Egg-Catching Contest

Inquiry Question

Can you design a container that can keep a raw egg from breaking when dropped from the ceiling?

Concept

Students will design and test a container that can keep a raw egg from breaking.

Purpose and Objectives

This is an example of a design activity that meets the math/science/technology standards (Standards 1, 3, and 6). Students will design and test a container that can keep a raw egg from breaking when dropped from seven or eight feet in the air.

Materials

- Soft packing materials such as Styrofoam, peanuts, cotton, paper towels, bubble wrap
- Creative devices such as Jello pudding, water, containers, pillow, and so on
- Materials students bring from home to finish their group's design.

Procedures

This technology activity should be preceded by a math and science unit on force and motion so that students are able to apply their knowledge of mathematics and science in their design process. Divide the class into groups of about four students each. Explain that each group is responsible for planning the egg-catching design. Emphasize creativity. The egg catcher must be twelve inches off the floor.

Explain the problem or challenge. Your group must work together to

- brainstorm ideas;
- sketch a design;
- formulate a rationale;
- assign group tasks—including setting up a cleanup crew;
- get materials;
- build the container;
- try several tests; and
- perform a class demonstration.

Evaluation, Completion, and/or Follow-up

The presentation will begin with a discussion of what the group has done to meet the challenge. Assessment for the egg catcher is not whether or not the egg broke but rather how they were able to share what they found out as they tried to solve the problem and prepared for a successful attempt. It's helpful to have the class make a video of the presentation. It can be viewed again by the designers and by parents, or it can be used in other class sessions in years to come.

Designing and Building a City (Upper Grades)

Inquiry Question

How are cities planned?

Concept

Among other things, city planning involves examining maps, collecting data, designing, and planning for construction.

Purpose and Objectives

This is an example of a design activity that meets the math/science/technology standards.

Another interesting problem for middle school students is to design and build a city. Students are instructed to design a city with an efficient road network. They must also create an election process that ensures the city council fairly represents all city residents. In addition, students must contact construction companies and make a plan for building their cities. To prepare for this challenge, students have to learn about routing graphs, which are used to plan routes for mail carriers and garbage carriers so they don't waste steps or gas unnecessarily. Contractors also use routing graphs to plan roads in new residential communities. Students collaborate in groups analyzing their decisions by writing a rationale for their design decisions. They must also make a fifteen-minute oral presentation to "sell" their cities. This project allows students to be creative in applying the science, math, and technology applications they've learned. Some students have created their cities on islands, on the moon . . . even underground.

Other Science and Math Ideas

Inquiry Question

What kind of devices can you create to make your life easier?

Concept

Creative ideas can be developed by everyone.

Purpose and Objectives

This is an example of a design activity that meets the math/science/technology standards.

Innovative ideas can be low tech. Some low-tech activities might include the following: (1) design a device to keep pencils from rolling off your desk, (2) create something that's easy to make that tastes good and would fit in your lunch box, (3) design a device that would shield your eyes from the sun, (4) create an instrument that would make lifting easier, and (5) design ways to save money on school supplies.

COLLABORATION AMONG MATH, SCIENCE, AND TECHNOLOGY EDUCATORS

The science and technology standards connect students to the designed world and introduce them to the laws of nature through their understanding of how technological objects and systems work. People have always invented tools to help them solve problems and to answer the many questions they have about their world. Just as scientists and engineers work in teams to get results, so students should work in teams that combine math, science, and engineering talents (Wenglinsky, 2005).

Getting the educational job done requires teachers who can help students from diverse backgrounds gain the competencies needed for identifying, analyzing, and solving mathematical, scientific, and technological problems. With the high-tech explosion of possibilities, it is important to remember that curriculum connections to the world of numbers and the natural world must be filtered through the mind of the teacher. It is also time to make sure that students who struggle with math, science, or technology become engaged with these subjects. Clearly, investment in "human ware" beats investment in "software" every time.

UNDERSTANDING TECHNOLOGICAL DESIGN

The science standards begin with the suggestion that students should learn to understand the design process and be able to solve simple design problems. The process is helped along the way if students develop the skills needed to creatively solve everyday problems with technology; it also helps if they are familiar with technological products and systems.

One way to foster innovation and creativity is to encourage learners to take two unrelated ideas or things and come up with new solutions, objects, or situations. To be able to do this it helps if you can look at the world as multiple objects mixed in multiple ways. Creative professionals in math, science, technology, and other subjects often go from looking at one thing from multiple perspectives to viewing multiple things mixed together in unpredictable ways.

It is usually best if students of all ages learn about math, science, and technology by firsthand experiences with technological tools similar to those used by accomplished experts. Although we pay close attention to digital technology, the math and science standards point out that young children should also see the technological products and systems found in the relatively low-tech world of zippers, can openers, and math manipulatives. Throughout the primary grades, students can use both low- and high-tech approaches to engage in projects that are appropriately challenging for them.

Even solving simple problems where they are trying to meet certain criteria, learners will find elements of math, science, and technology that can be powerful aids. At higher grade levels, lessons can include examples of technological achievements where math and science have played a part. Students can also be encouraged to examine where technical advances have contributed directly to scientific progress. To consider the other side of the coin, students can go online and find examples of where the technological products of math and science have done harmful things—like damaging the environment or taking away jobs.

Children and young adults should have many experiences that involve math, science, and all kinds of technology. It might be as simple as measuring and weighing various objects on a balance scale. This can teach math and science skills such as comparing, estimating, predicting, and recording data. What is the technology connection? A scale is one of the relatively simple technological tools used in mathematics and science for measuring mass or weight.

Too frequently, however, teachers forget to mention the technological connection. Whether it's simple or complex, bathroom scales or hot new computers, technology is a ubiquitous part of our day-to-day world. And it's as misunderstood as it is hard to escape.

Students can be motivated by studying existing technology products to determine their function—identifying the problems the device might solve, the materials used in its construction, and how well it does what it is supposed to do. A low-tech device, like a vegetable or cheese grater, is an example of a simple object that young children can investigate—figuring out what it does, how it helps people, and what problems it might solve and cause. Such a problem provides an excellent opportunity for directing attention to a specific, yet simple technology.

In the early elementary grades, many tasks can be designed around the familiar items in the home, school, and community. In the early grades, problems should be clear and have only one or two solutions that do not require a great deal of preparation time or complicated assembly.

As the standards make clear, children can learn a great deal about math, science, and technology from the low-tech *and* the high-tech ends of the spectrum.

Many curriculum programs and some state guidelines suggest that teachers integrate math and science with digital technology and examine related social issues. The suggestion is that this be done in a way that encourages multidisciplinary analysis of problems that are relevant to the students' world. To get a little history into the process, it is also useful to examine many of the good (and bad) technology-assisted events of the past. How many electronic communication tools available today weren't around ten years ago? Thirty years ago? Point out that technology is in a constant process of adjustment, innovation, and surprise.

New media surprises, like the iPhone, are already an integral part of the lives of young people. In many of today's classrooms, computers and other devices tend to be used to make both routine and more inventive activities more interesting. In tomorrow's schools, digital tools will permeate the curriculum—and they will do so in ways that create new contexts for inquiry and problem solving.

A sequence of five stages is a good way to approach the problem-solving process: (1) identifying and stating the problem, (2) designing an approach to solving the problem, (3) implementing and arriving at a solution, (4) evaluating results, and (5) communicating the problem, design, and solution. In keeping with the math, science, and technology standards documents, teachers are increasingly encouraging students to design problems and conduct technological investigations in ways that incorporate interesting issues and dilemmas.

By using a variety of materials and technologies for problem solving and inquiry, students can come to recognize (as John Dewey and others have suggested) that education is more than preparing for life; it is life itself. In a world permeated by technology, students will do better in school and in life if they are familiar with technology and have an understanding of the subject.

Those who graduate with a better technology education are likely to improve their choices as consumers, employ technology more effectively in their daily lives, and make better citizen choices about technological issues in society (Peason & Young, 2002). In 2000, the International Technology Education Association (ITEA) published *Standards for Technological Literacy: Content for the Study of Technology.*

AN OVERVIEW OF ITEA'S *STANDARDS* FOR TECHNOLOGICAL LITERACY

Theme 1: Nature of Technology

- Characteristics and scope of technology
- Core concepts of technology
- Relationships among technologies and connections to other subjects

Theme 2: Technology and Society

- Cultural, social, economic, and political effects of technology
- Effects of technology on the environment
- Role of society in the development and use of technology
- Influence of technology on history

Theme 3: Design Processes

- Attributes of design
- Engineering design
- Role of research, development, invention, innovation, and experimentation in problem solving

Theme 4: Abilities for a Technological World

- Apply the design process
- Use and maintain technological products and systems
- Assess the impact of products and systems

Theme 5: The Designed World (Knowledge in Specific Technological Fields)

- Medical
- Agricultural and biotechnology
- Information and communication
- Transportation
- Manufacturing
- Construction

ACTIVITIES FOR UNDERSTANDING COMMUNICATIONS TECHNOLOGY

Activity 1: Communications Time Line (Upper Grades)

Inquiry Question

How have communications changed over time?

Concept

History influences how people communicate. The ways in which people communicate with each other have changed throughout history. In ancient days, cave painting conveyed messages and created meaning for people.

For centuries, storytelling and oral language served as the primary means of communicating information. Handwritten manuscripts were the first written for communication, followed more recently by the printing press, telegraph, typewriter, telephone, radio, television, computers, and video cell phone. The list could go on.

Purpose and Objectives

This is an example of a design activity that meets the math/science/technology standards (Standards 1, 2, 3, 5, and 6).

Through this activity, students will research the history of communications technology and create a time line in their math/science journal. This activity allows students to collect as many actual objects as possible or their representations for display. They will provide a written explanation about these communications devices and talk and share ideas with others, answering any questions the class raises.

Materials

Reference books; science/math journals; and communication devices from home, grandparents, community, or elsewhere.

Procedure

1. Have students conduct research on the history of communications technology and create a time line. Have them put their notes in their math/science journal.
2. Encourage students to assemble a communications time line project for display, using as many actual objects or their representations as possible.
3. Remind students that each time period needs to have some examples of the actual objects used and a written explanation about these communications devices.

Evaluation, Extension

1. Direct students to choose a communications technique from the past. Teachers may wish to divide students into groups according to interests and assign each group a certain time period or technological tool used for communication.
2. Direct groups to orally (and perhaps graphically) present their communication tool to the class.
3. Teachers may extend the project by having students project what communications of the future will look like.

Activity 2: Create a Water Clock (Grade 3 and Up)

Inquiry Question

How do clocks work?

Concept

Clocks keep track of time. Time is often a difficult concept for children to grasp. People have recorded the passage of time throughout history.

Purpose and Objectives

This is an example of a design activity that meets the math/science/technology standards (Standards 1, 2, 3, 5, and 6).

This activity involves children in time measurement by using a number of old and new technological tools. Students will learn how to measure time using a variety of clocks.

Materials

- a variety of large cans, plastic bottles, and plastic containers
- a collection of corks or plugs
- modeling clay
- scissors or knife
- hammer and nail with large head
- math and science journal

Procedures

Have students collect a variety of large cans, plastic bottles, and plastic containers. You may wish to help them make a small hole in the bottom of the metal containers with either a hammer and large nail or in the plastic containers using a scissors or a knife (try to make all of the holes in the containers the same size). Instruct students to make a clay plug or a small cork to fit the hole. Have students fill the containers with water, then release the plugs and compare the times of each container. Encourage students to guess which one will empty first.

Evaluation, Follow-up

1. Have students choose common jobs that can be timed with water clocks.
2. Encourage students to make a list of things that can be timed with a water clock.

3. Instruct students to hypothesize what the effect of different sized holes is on the water drip process.
4. Have students use a digital clock to determine how much water flows out in one minute's time from their water clock.
5. Ask students to design a system to mark their water clock to determine the time without measuring the water each time.
6. Ask students if they can make a clock another way.
7. Have students write a program for a computer to record time.

Follow-up Questions

Instruct students to respond to these questions in their math/science journal:

- Why are clocks so important to the industrial age?
- How are clocks used as metaphors?
- Encourage students to speculate on the future of clocks and their role in the future.

Activity 3: Hypothesis Testing (Grades 4 and Up)

Inquiry Question

How do I find out?

Concept

This technology awareness activity is designed to get students involved in the historic role of technology in today's society.

Purpose and Objectives

Students will conduct inquiry in trying to discover what technological devices are being presented. Students will reinforce their skills of questioning, observing, communicating, and making inferences. This is an example of a design activity that meets the math/science/technology standards (Standards 1, 2, 3, 5, and 6).

Materials

Instruct students to bring in a paper bag containing the following:

- one item that no one would be able to recognize (an old tool of their grandfather's, for example)
- one item that some people may be able to identify
- one common item that everyone would recognize

Procedure

1. Divide students into small groups. Tell students that all items in their bags should be kept secret.
2. Give students the following directions:
   a. There will be no talking in the first part of this activity.
   b. You are to exchange bags with someone else in your group.
   c. You may then open the bag, remove one item, and write down what you think that item is. Examine each item carefully. Write your reaction to how you feel about this item, what you think it may be used for, and which category this item falls into (common item, one no one would recognize, etc.).
3. Repeat with each of the items in your bag.
4. Exchange bags with other groups and go through the same procedure.

Evaluation, Completion, and Follow-up

When everyone has finished examining their bag of articles and written their responses, meet back together in your group and explain what you have discovered in your bag. Encourage class speculation, questions, and guesses about unidentified items. The student who brought the unknown tool or article should be responsible for answering the questions posed but should not give away the identity until all guesses and hypotheses have been raised.

When students engage in formal and informal math, science, or technology activities, they develop and use a number of science process skills. From the early childhood years onward, children use the skills of observing, classifying, measuring, estimating, inferring, predicting, and communicating. It is best to develop these skills in the context of social interaction; so it's best to pay attention to teamwork skills during scientific inquiry and mathematical problem solving. To encourage creative and innovative thinking, teams need to be small, dynamic, and flexible—and they also need to stay focused on the content of the lesson.

Suggestions for teachers and parents follow:

- Praise effort more than achievement.
- Teach delayed gratification.
- Limit reprimands.
- Use praise to stimulate curiosity.

At home or at school, a bad environment suppresses creative and innovative development.

SCAFFOLDING

When a student falters in a lesson, a teacher can help just enough to make sure the student accomplishes a task. Later, the student or small group will be able to do the work on their own.

Steps

- Observe to figure out what the student or pair of students is trying to do.
- Ask the students what they intend to do. (Getting verbal input shows respect for ideas.)
- Comment on the student actions in a way that shows you are paying attention.
- Scaffold verbally or through action to provide possible ways to solve a problem.
- Once the process of completing the task is under way, step back from input.
- When work is done, comment on the accomplishment. (Your comment will add value to the new skills.)

The structure can be differentiated in a way that supports what's needed to accomplish the task. The number of steps needed to solve the problem can be reduced (or increased) so that interest is maintained and frustration is avoided. Peers can be very helpful in the scaffolding process. The teacher focuses on what the student is doing, what they need in order to learn, and gives only enough help to overcome roadblocks.

FINDING VIDEO CLIPS ONLINE

Using multimedia is a good way to activate prior knowledge and differentiate mental models in a way that helps a wide range of students acquire new knowledge. Some suggested resources follow:

A9
http://a9.com
This search engine is from Amazon.com and searches for images, movies, blogs, books, and other websites.

Creative Commons
http://creativecommons.org

This is a nonprofit search engine that searches flexible copyright use for anyone putting together a creative package that requires video, graphics, sounds, or publications.

Google Video
http://video.google.com
This search engine looks for video clips using the keywords you enter.

The Internet Archive
www.archive.org
This resource has video clips from the entire twentieth century. A feature called the Wayback Machine is particularly popular with students.

Discovery Education Streaming
http://streaming.discoveryeducation.com
This is a good educational video collection and a good advance organizer for starting a learning activity.

By creating original multimedia stories, students can't help but see the inner processes of media. The new concept of literacy is bound to involve "reading" and "writing" in multiple media formats, connecting to the curriculum, and integrating the result into a meaningful whole (Ohler, 2007).

Many teachers who are unfamiliar with multimedia technology overestimate the difficulty of getting students started. Just put them with a partner and ask them to play with a couple of sites first. The next step is figuring out an interesting project. Another approach is to have students explore these sites as homework; when they come to class, they can team up and explore where to go in a way that connects to the curriculum.

GOING ON A VIRTUAL FIELD TRIP

It's best if students go someplace by boarding a bus with a permission slip, a bag lunch, and a buddy system (so that nobody gets lost). But what can you do if there is no money for a school bus or if the site is too far away? A virtual field trip may be the answer. Suggestions follow:

- Make sure that the virtual field trip ties in with the curriculum.
- Start by making sure that everyone has a partner; if the numbers don't work out evenly, there can be one group of three students.
- Be sure that each pair has a goal and is looking for ideas, not just different places.
- Consider having students keep a journal or answer some questions about their online travels.

- You might want to send a note home so that parents know what's going on.
- Continue the work off-line by planning at least part of a lesson around the virtual field trip.

(Making a virtual visit is also a good way to get ready for a real visit.)

It would be a shame to cancel a real visit that is a reasonable drive from school. But virtual field trips can be used more easily—and they can take students places that they couldn't reach in any other way. It's also a good way to motivate students who are hard to reach in other ways.

DIGITAL TECHNOLOGY IN TODAY'S CLASSROOM

Teachers and students may wish to communicate with peers, parents, and the larger world community. However, we suggest that teachers not accept instant messages from students; reserve your personal e-mail address for professional activities. Teachers can, however, use the full range of available technology to enhance their productivity and improve their professional practice. Lifelong learning and personal change are facts of life in the twenty-first century. When teachers are supported and well prepared, they can walk in the world with such confidence and enthusiasm that they don't have to fear the unhappiness of change.

New technology is constantly changing math, science, and technology instruction by altering the general academic environment and providing new opportunities for students to create knowledge for themselves. This encourages students to learn by doing—going beyond the "telling" model of instruction that so many students find problematical.

Digital technology can also serve as a vehicle for inquiry-based classrooms—giving students access to data, experiences with simulations, and the possibility for creating models of fundamental math/science/technology processes. Like a good teacher, today's technology has, at least, the possibility of increasing everybody's capacity to learn.

What about early childhood education? In the primary grades, technology has gone beyond simply being enrichment or an add-on to the curriculum. Digital technology can help younger children view things in their world from different perspectives. With a digital camera or microscope attachment to the computer, learners can view and communicate close-ups of plant and animal life.

Also, children in the lower grades can hypothesize, experiment, and work together to solve problems with a variety of technological tools. At any age, when students listen to the views of others, they stretch their concepts, consider different points of view, and recast ideas to communicate and advance their understanding.

Moving into the upper elementary and middle school grades, in one technologically savvy sixth-grade classroom we visited, students were involved with software and Internet website evaluation. The teacher was using Smart Board technology to help the students with note taking and to preserve student ideas. One struggling student and his partner were encouraged to write in and highlight the text. All of the students were working in pairs to construct flow charts and graphic organizers.

The homework question of the week was "What is the role of media in our society?" A more intriguing and controversial question was "How do you have a just society when genetics is so unjust?" The teacher made sure that everyone had an online study partner. And they made sure the students knew how to prepare a summary of their homework discussions for the teacher. Not many of us could juggle all this and integrate the result into the curriculum. But with time, practice, and a little in-service training, teachers less familiar with technology can easily become aware of the general issues and make the appropriate match between the problems they face and potential technological support.

Digital technology is transforming our educational and social environment so fast that we haven't had the time to think carefully about the best way to use it. Like everyone else, teachers are consumers of technology and they need to be able to judge critically the quality and usefulness of the electronic possibilities springing up around them.

Many people outside of school think that life today is moving too fast—hyped up with wireless laptops, netbooks, cell phones with TV shows, podcasts, blogs, BlackBerries, and instant messages. They should try to imagine what it is like to be a teacher with struggling students, new curriculum choices, political demands, standardized tests, and whizbang technologies swirling around them.

THE VALUE OF INSIGHTS AND IDEAS

Throughout history, there has been human conflict over things like land and natural resources. Now there is as much attention given to the value of more abstract ideas. The Internet is, after all, an abstraction. And the value of Google exceeds the value of Boeing, Lockheed, and General Motors. As recently as twenty years ago, the Internet was a dusty relic of the Cold War and Google was way out beyond the horizon. But in an age of constant surprises, old assumptions got thrown out and new approaches were embraced. Sometimes, the technology worked out and sometimes it didn't. Either way, adapting quickly was—and is—the key to success.

Here is a way to think about insights, new ideas, and innovation: An insight is likely to come as a quick flash as you think about something or discuss it with others. An idea might be thought of as a proposition for action that has a beginning, a middle, and an end. As you work to implement a new idea, it may become an innovation. The end result is often a new concept, product, or service.

Teachers, parents, and various media can significantly affect how children and young adults respond to a complex world in which changes don't always take place in a smooth, linear progression. More often than not, major changes happen in sequences of fast (occasionally catastrophic) events. Technology education matters. Skills acquired in analyzing the information about quickly changing situations (gathered from old and new media) can help (Ramo, 2009).

What students learn from critically and creatively examining any visually intensive medium will apply as more advanced multimedia devices come online. Whether it is television, the Internet, or just about any other platform, students' social, educational, and family context influences the messages they get, how they use media, and how "literate" they are as users (Kress, 2003). To become critical and imaginative thinkers who can understand conflicting media messages, students should being able to

- understand the grammar and syntax as expressed in different presentation forms;
- develop ways of looking at problems that focus more on context and less on reductive answers;
- analyze the pervasive appeals of advertising;
- compare similar presentations or those with similar purposes in different media;
- identify values in language, characterization, conflict resolution, and sound/visual images;
- identify elements in dramatic presentations associated with the concepts of plot, story line, theme, characterizations, motivation, program formats, and production values; and
- utilize strategies for the management of duration of time online, viewing, and program choices.

Whether it's understanding media or contemplating the uncertain nature of a rapidly changing world, it's a little like getting into good physical condition—you have to begin very early. And you have to keep at it.

PROVIDING GOOD ROLE MODELS

Teachers and parents can structure activities that affect the interest of young people in media messages and help them learn how to process media-supplied information. They can also help youngsters get used to the notion that, in the twenty-first century, uncertainty and indeterminacy are givens. Modeling good behavior, explaining content, and showing how the program content relates to authentic daily concerns are just a few examples of how adults can provide positive possibilities for the use of media and information. Adults can also exhibit an informed response, pointing out misleading messages and taking care not to build curiosity for undesirable programming.

The viewing and computer-using habits of families play a large role in determining how children approach media. For example, the length of time parents spend watching television, the kinds of programs viewed, and the reactions of parents and siblings toward programming messages all have a large influence on children. If adults read and there are books, magazines, and newspapers around the house, children will pay more attention to print. Influencing what young people view on television and the Internet may be done with rules about what may or may not be watched, interactions during viewing, and the modeling of certain content choices.

When it comes to the Internet, we suggest having children and young adults use their computer in a space where parents can keep an eye on them. What about television? Whether co-viewing or not, the viewing choices of adults in a child's life (parents, teachers, etc.) set an example for them. If parents are heavy watchers of public television or news programming, then children are more likely to respond favorably to this content. If parents use a pared-down version of Windows 7 on a $250 netbook computer, their children are more likely to do the same.

Influencing the settings in which children attend to media is a crucial factor in productive use. For example, turning the computer or TV set off during meals sets a family priority. Families can also seek a more open and equal approach to choosing Internet sites or television shows—interacting before, during, and after the viewing. Parents can also organize formal or informal activities outside the house that provide alternatives to computer games, Internet use, or TV viewing.

It is increasingly clear that the education of children is a shared responsibility. Parents need connections with what's going on in the schools. But it is *teachers* who will be the ones called upon to make the educational connections entwining varieties of print and visual media with science, mathematics, or technology education. It is possible to explore any medium in a way that encourages students to become intelligent consumers. The activities that follow are designed to be used with upper elementary and middle school students.

QUESTIONS TO START THE DISCUSSION

1. What is your favorite website, television show, and movie?
2. What kind of information, show, or movie is it?

3. What are the formal features of your choices?
4. What are the most appealing elements of each?
5. What do you know about how each medium constructs their "stories"?
6. What are some of the formal and informal structures of the Internet, movie industry, and television broadcasting?
7. What are the values in these mass-produced "programs," and how do they change our shared experiences as a people?

Fifteen years ago, our shared experiences almost always included books and newspapers. Now, only the more educated members of our society spend a great deal of time with the printed word.

ACTIVITIES THAT CAN HELP STUDENTS MAKE SENSE OF TELEVISION

1. Help Students Critically View What They Watch

Decoding visual stimuli and learning from visual images require practice. Seeing an image does not automatically ensure learning from it. Students must be guided in decoding and looking critically at what they view. One technique is to have students "read" the image on various levels. Students identify individual elements and classify them into various categories, then relate the whole to their own experiences, drawing inferences, and creating new conceptualizations from what they have learned.

Encourage students to look at the plot and story line. Identify the message of the program. What symbols (camera techniques, motion sequences, setting, lighting, etc.) does the program use to make its message? What does the director do to arouse audience emotion and participation in the story? What metaphors and symbols are used? (These activities are examples of the design activity that meets the math/science/technology standards.)

2. Compare Print and Video Messages

Have students follow a current event on the evening news and compare it to the same event written in a major newspaper. A question for discussion may be as follows: how do the major newspapers influence what appears on a national network's news program? Encourage comparisons between both media. What are the strengths and weaknesses of each? What are the reasons behind the different presentations of a similar event?

3. Evaluate Viewing Habits

After compiling a list of their favorite programs, assign students to analyze the reasons for their popularity and examine the messages these programs send to their audience. Do the same for favorite books, magazines, newspapers, films, songs, and computer programs. Look for similarities and differences among the different forms of media.

4. Use Video for Instruction

Use a VCR, DVD player, or computer projection equipment to make frequent use of three- to five-minute video segments to illustrate different points. This is usually better than showing long segments. For example, teachers can show a five-minute segment from a movie to illustrate how one scene uses foreshadowing or music to set up the next scene.

5. Analyze Advertising Messages

Advertisements provide a wealth of examples for illustrating media messages. Move students progressively from advertisements in print to television commercials, allowing them to locate features (such as packaging, color, and images) that influence consumers and often distort reality. Analyze and discuss commercials in children's programs: How many minutes of TV or Internet ads appear in an hour? How have toy or game manufacturers exploited the medium? What is the broadcasters' or developer's role? What should be done about it?

6. Create a Scrapbook of Media Clippings

Have students keep a scrapbook of newspaper and magazine clippings on electronic media. Paraphrase, draw a picture, or map out a personal interpretation of the articles. Share these with other students.

7. Create New Images from the Old

Have students take rather mundane photographs and multiply the image, or combine it with others, in a way that makes them interesting. The artist David Hockney calls this a "Joiner." Through the act of observing, it is possible to build a common body of experiences, humor, feeling, and originality. And through collaborative efforts, students can expand on ideas and make the group process come alive.

8. Use Debate for Critical Thought

Debating is a communications model that can serve as a lively facilitator for concept building. Taking a current and relevant topic and formally debating it can serve as an important speech/language extension. For example, the class can discuss how mass media can support political tyranny, public conformity, or the technological enslavement of society. The discussion can serve as a blend of social studies, science, and humanities studies. You can also build the process of writing or videotaping from the brainstorming stage to the final production.

9. Include Newspapers, Magazines, Literature, and Electronic Media (Like Brief Television News Clips) in Daily Class Activities

Use of the media and literature can enliven classroom discussion of current conflicts and dilemmas. Neither squeamish nor politically correct, these sources of information provide readers with something to think and talk about. And they can present the key conflicts and dilemmas of our time in ways that allow students to enter the discussion.

These stimulating sources of information can help the teacher structure lessons that go beyond facts to stimulate reading, critical thinking, and thoughtful discussion. By not concealing adult disagreements, everyone can take responsibility for promoting understanding—engaging others in moral reflection and providing a coherence and focus that help turn controversies into advantageous educational experiences.

HOW TO CHOOSE COMPUTER SOFTWARE

Most teachers subscribe to a number of professional journals, and just about every school staff room has dozens of instruction-oriented magazines. Many have all kinds of practical suggestions that are simple enough to put in the hands of upper grade students so they can help with selections. Also, some teacher magazines regularly give software reviews that can keep both you and your students up to date.

Whether it's on paper or online, many educational and most technology magazines often publish an annotated list of what their critics take to be the best new programs of the year. Even some of the old reliables have been improved and put on CD-ROM or made available on the Internet. Also, district supervisors may have a list of what they think will work at your grade level. You can even get your class directly involved in the software evaluation process. This helps your students reach the goal of understanding the educational purpose of the activity.

We like to start our technology workshops by having participants work in pairs to review a few good programs that a school district is likely to have. As you and your students go about choosing programs for the classroom, the following checklist may prove useful.

Software Checklist

1. Can the software be used easily by two students working together? (Graphic and spoken instructions help.)

2. What is the program trying to teach, and how does it fit into the curriculum?
3. Does the software encourage students to experiment and think creatively about what they are doing?
4. Is the program lively and interesting?
5. Does it allow students to collaborate, explore, and laugh?
6. Is the software technically sophisticated enough to build on multisensory ways of learning?
7. Is there any way to assess student performance?
8. What activities, materials, or manipulatives would extend the skills taught by this program?

The bottom line is *do you and your students like it?* We suggest that teachers reserve their final judgment until they observe students using the program. Don't expect perfection. But if it doesn't build on the unique capacities of the computer, then you may just have an expensive electronic workbook that will not be of much use to anybody. With today's interactive multimedia programs, there is every reason to expect science and math programs that can invite students to interact with creatures and phenomena from the biological and physical universe.

Students can move from the past to the future and actively inquire about everything from experiments with dangerous substances to simulated interaction with long dead scientists. Just don't leave out experiments with real chemicals and experiences with live human beings.

Good educational software often tracks individual progress over time and gives special attention to problem areas. Most of what you find on the Internet doesn't do that. Free Internet offerings have cut into the sale of educational software and diminished the quality. Another change is a tendency to move away from the computer platform and put educational programming on all kinds of gadgets. Even *Children's Software Review* has changed its name to *Children's Technology Review*. One of their links, www. littleclickers.com, is a good site for finding educational games available on the Internet.

NEW MEDIA REALITIES CREATED
BY NETWORKING TECHNOLOGIES

"Collective intelligence" is one of the terms used to describe a future cell phone–using world where people are permanently connected to anything and everything. Profit-seeking companies are excited about the possibility of such a network because having a record of our behavior ("reality mining") allows them to create carefully tailored products that can be delivered exactly when they think people will buy them. Even consumers' wallets are being integrated into mobile phones. Just tap the phone on a wireless store terminal and you pay the bill. But whether it's networked reality mining or digital wallets, *user beware.*

Fortunately, there are positive tech-centered learning opportunities. There are studies that point to potential benefits when students and teachers use computer-based technology and information networks (Ohler, 2007). The following are examples:

- Computer-based simulations and laboratories can be downloaded in support of the standards.
- Students can more easily become involved in active participatory learning.
- Networking technology, like the Internet, can help bring schools and homes closer together.
- Technology and telecommunications can help include students with a wide range of disabilities in regular classrooms.
- Distance learning, through networks like the Internet, can extend the learning community beyond the classroom walls.
- The Internet may help teachers continue to learn—while sharing problems/solutions with colleagues around the world.

Various digital devices have gained enough users to be a force for change, including changing the way teachers teach and the way students learn. To make sure things move in the right direction, it is important to control the environment so that students don't end up doing instant messaging or downloading music onto school computers. In classrooms where computers are used, one of the first things that teachers learn is when to say "computers off"—or "screens down" if learners are using laptops. Remember, anything that diminishes attention and rapport with others gets in the way of deep learning.

Since the Internet is rarely censored, it is important to supervise student work or use a program that blocks the most objectionable websites. We suggest that teachers keep an eye on what students are doing and make sure that the classroom is off-line when a substitute teacher is in. A program like NetNanny is one way to prevent children from accessing inappropriate material. Just as with libraries and bookstores, it is important not to restrict the free flow of information and ideas. But there can be a children's section without bringing everyone down to the intellectual level of a seven-year-old.

In today's world, many children grow up interacting with electronic media as much as they do with print or people. At school, digital technology makes it relatively easy to engage even the most reluctant learner. But does this mean that students are learning anything meaningful or that they are making good use of either educational *or* leisure time?

The Internet, like other electronic media, can distract students from face-to-face interaction with peers—inhibiting important group and physical exercise activities. Still, although the future may be bumpy, it doesn't have to be gloomy. Good use of any learning tool depends on the strength and capacity of teachers. The best results occur when it is informed educators who are making instructional decisions, rather than simply following a path set by the technology itself.

Harmonizing the present and an even more technologically intensive future has a lot to do with improving the schools. Digital tools have great promise, but anyone who thinks that technological approaches will solve most educational problems is mistaken. It's important to turn the volume down on the cacophony of conflicting directives and specious conjecture about the educational future and focus on what is known about instruction.

Research frequently points to what works—including technology, standards, textbooks, activities, and assessment. But when it comes to actually *doing what works*, the most important factor affecting how much students learn is *teachers*.

USING DIGITAL TOOLS TO EXPLORE QUESTIONS AND DILEMMAS

Making good use of technology requires going beyond using it as an electronic version of the same old thing. At its best, technology can deepen subject matter understanding and promote innovative thinking. Digital technology can also open up new and unique possibilities that take students well beyond textbooks and worksheets. Among other things, it can amplify the energy and the intellectual curiosity that are needed to learn more on a daily basis.

Technology opens up possibilities for moving schools in the direction of being more responsive, modern, and effective. There are also many ways it can help teachers. For example, a Webcam can be used to record a difficult lesson; the next step would be to put it up on the Internet and get some suggestions from other educators. Students can take a similar approach when they come up with difficult questions; remember, if they can't get answers, their curiosity is diminished the next time around. In addition, digital tools can help learners get around what's blocking answers—while at the same time, increasing motivation (Buckingham, 2007).

For students to successfully sail through the crosscurrents of our transitional age, teachers need to make sure they are given the opportunity for important learning. There are times when digital technology can help; at other times, it may be best to get it out of the way. A lot depends on the nature of the digital device and the structure of the curriculum.

New mobile products are coming out all the time, and polite use is hard for some to figure out. As irritating as those obsessed with handheld devices and computer-generated e-mail may be, no one can completely dismiss the technology. Here are some suggestions for educators and young adults:

- Set times of the day when you check messages; at other times, put devices away.
- Text messages lead to more text messages; use the phone or show up in person.
- If you have a handheld device with you at a meeting, place it face down and off.
- Set up an e-mail filter that keeps out ads and low priority messages.
- Avoid replying to messages on evenings or weekends.
- Make sure that instant answers are not expected.
- Be sure that *you* (not the device) are in control.

At any age, it's important to have some rules of the road so that using digital devices shows respect for those around you.

QUESTIONS, POSSIBILITIES, AND PROBLEMS IN CYBERSPACE

Fairly recent media, like YouTube and Facebook, are having a major effect on popular culture. In a digital era of new cognitive models, social networking websites, and freewheeling video downloads, one person's voice can occasionally have as much power as a TV network. When a new medium arrives on the scene, there is usually the same reaction: What is it going to take the place of? What is it going to do to culture and morals? Is it going to make us sick?

Some of the pluses and minuses of digital technologies may be found in earlier media. For example, when television first gained a central place in the American consciousness, the sociologist Leo Bogart wrote that it was a "neutral instrument in human hands. It is and does what people want."[4] The same thing might be said about today's multimedia and telecommunications technologies.

Problems in Cyberspace

- Intelligence agencies secretly embedding malicious code on computer chips when they are manufactured—allowing them to take control sometime in the future.

- Trojan horses: code embedded in legitimate hardware or software.
- Viruses and worms: software that infects other files, often reproducing on its own and spreading throughout a network.
- Bot-nets: networks of infected computers that can be controlled remotely to generate spam; they can also be used to coordinate a massive assault.
- Denial of service attacks: causing a website or network to crash by overwhelming it with fake requests.
- Scanning and sniffing: exploring a network looking for weak points, searching for passwords, intercepting data, and looking for other information.
- Phishing and vishing: using fake e-mail, websites, or voice-over-the-Internet technology to trick people into revealing information.

A good activity is to have learners collaboratively explore and explain some of these digital dragons. Add to the list. See if student pairs or small groups can elaborate on cyber attack strategies, come up with examples, and briefly present the whole class with ways to take defensive action.

Technological change is more than a random phenomenon; usually, there is a cause and effect relationship. Rapid changes in information technology are resulting in less of a difference among the television screen, the computer screen, and cell phone–linked networks. It's becoming a steady stream of fast-moving, crowd-sourced innovation and collective creativity.

As we venture out onto the bumpy electronic road ahead, we should remember the words of T. S. Eliot: "Time present and time past are both perhaps contained in time future. And time future contained in time past."[5]

DIFFERENTIATION, THE INTERNET, AND INTERESTING GROUP WORK

Education is a regulation of the process of coming to share in the social consciousness.

—John Dewey[6]

Differentiation, collaborative learning, and the Internet are natural partners. To access a good sample of recommended Internet resources, try www.filamentality.com and search for "DI Using Technology." But whether you are online or offline, it's important to remember that students come to whatever they are doing or reading with different levels of prior knowledge. To find good activities, we often use WebQuests.

There are investigative activities on the Internet that are educator created and peer reviewed. A few free examples are www.webquest.org and www. discoveryschool.com. If you are willing to pay for a subscription, www. webquestdirect.com.au is a good service.

Here is a simple lesson for mixed-ability groups: everyone reads or does the same math, science, or technology problem, activity, or section of text. Each student finds a partner and does some Internet research that they will bring back to the small group. We, sometimes, have upper grade students explore the medium itself by going online to read reviews of related books. *The Google Story* by David Vise and *The Search* by John Battelle are good examples. The Google Book Search Library Project has made a vast number of books available online.

Information from the *outside* world is readily available for students; it is even possible to "Google" human genes to get information about the world *inside*. Disruptive technologies, like Google and the iPod, are good topics for student exploration. They shake things up by changing the way that students, adults, and businesses think and operate.

When it comes to encouraging innovative thoughtfulness in the class-room, it is important to provide multiple (differentiated) options for accessing information. Working with peers to engage content with digital tools is part of the process. The goal is to inspire learners to be thinkers and innovators. So, it is important to go beyond chalk, teacher talk, and printed materials in ways that build on divergent thinking and group dynamics.

Collaborative groups help strengthen the classroom community and do a better job of engaging the full spectrum of students. When students feel that "we're all together," it encourages them to take on different roles, share resources, and help each other learn.

We owe everything to human creativity. Everything that lasts, changes our lives, that emerges from what was once the unimaginable has its roots in that initial spark of innovation.

—Joshua Cooper Ramo (2009)[7]

COLLABORATION, DIFFERENTIATION, AND IMAGINATIVE ENGAGEMENT

After discussions in small collaborative groups, projects or work assign-ments can be brought back to the whole class so each group can share their findings. Sometimes, a group may want to put their findings online or post their book reviews at www.amazon.com. Wikipedia has open editing, so students can put some things there. This online encyclopedia is very timely, but the accuracy is mixed. So, we tell students that it's a good starting point but that it shouldn't be their only source.

When students are actively engaged with ideas and other students, the natural power of teamwork accommodates more types of learning than the old chalk and teacher talk model. It has always been true that, when interesting questions are raised in learning groups, those involved tend to lead each other forward. Struggling students may need to take conscious steps to activate prior knowledge. This can be done as a small group reviews what's been covered out loud and on paper.

Collaborative learning of this type is effective because the framework of the strategy is good for all students. The research also suggests that somewhat collaborative learning groups result in more cross-cultural friendships and have some positive effect on intergroup relations. With an increasingly diverse group of students, learning to advance through the intersection of different points of view is more important than ever.

New technologies give teachers powerful tools for offering a customized curriculum in a social context. Amazon's Kindle reader is but one example of an e-book that can hold a small library of books. Another product, Thinking Readers, provides built-in supports that include differentiated learning and reciprocal (student to student) teaching.

We like using "know—want to know—learned" (KWL) charts with both paper and electronic books. It has three columns labeled: *know, want to know*, and *learned*. Just before reading, two students work together to put down what they know about a subject. In the second column, they write what they want to know. After they explored a math- or science-related passage, they write what they learned in a third column.

This builds on prior knowledge and teamwork. It also brings a focus to the work. To communicate the work to everybody, we have student teams put their work on large pieces of paper so they can be taped up, explained, and seen by everybody in a whole-class discussion.

While aiming high, teachers have to be realistic about what children and young adults can achieve. To help all students, teachers need to focus on the concepts they want to teach. The next step is figuring out how different kinds of learners are going to show an understanding of what's covered. Digital technology can give students more control over their own learning. It can also enhance collaborative learning, with students constructing meaning and understanding by interacting with others (Adams, 2001).

Digital media has great promise for keeping students creatively engaged in learning. But differentiation matters—and it's just as bad to say that Jane is bored as to say that Johnny can't learn. So, it is important that teachers provide extra enrichment for their high-achieving students so they stay challenged and their parents stay cooperative.

Contrary to public opinion, intelligent people are not always the most innovative thinkers; for one thing, they may be tempted to use their abilities to support a particular position rather than constructively exploring questions and problems. Creating a more innovative classroom environment requires paying attention to developing the innovative and creative potential that all children possess.

Innovative people vary in their natural ability levels, motivation, and interests. However, they may share certain characteristics. They tend to be

- flexible in their thinking,
- curious and resourceful,
- able to solve difficult problems,
- comfortable outside traditional boundaries,
- good at seeing new implications,
- able to synthesize different possibilities, and
- self-confident and willing to take risks (Brown, 2007)

Sparking innovative insights requires everyone from teachers to scientists to find ways of inspiring young people to create and innovate so they can become inventors and makers of things. After all, students can be more than just consumers of something someone else developed.

MATH, SCIENCE, AND TECHNOLOGY STANDARDS: PROMISE AND PITFALLS

National standards have brought more coordination, consistency, coherence, and focus to math, science, and technology instruction. All three standards documents have spelled out approaches that involve creating environments where teachers and students work together as active learners. Assessment and learning are viewed as flip sides of the same coin.

The standards also address the need for professional development that goes beyond technical proficiencies to provide teachers with opportunities to develop theoretical and practical understanding. Meaningful staff development is aimed at helping teachers develop their professional habits and practices. The ultimate goal is to help teachers become lifelong learners so they constantly improve their ability to help students learn more effectively.

Professional development will help teachers who feel challenged by students who grew up in a digital world. In spite of generational differences, today's students come into the classroom with very different technology-related experience, attitudes, and expectations. Many spend more time on the Internet than they do watching television. Technological skills are important, but even the most tech savvy students have to learn how to use a wider range of resources when gathering information. To appreciate the limitations of digital technology, everyone must also be able to identify, access, evaluate, and use the best resources at hand, regardless of format.

You don't have to be a computer technician to lead students into a digital-intensive future. However, you do have to know how to orchestrate learning conditions in a way that brings out the best in everybody, effectively managing students' time, talents, and productivity. This means implementing a variety of instructional and grouping strategies in a way that meets the diverse needs of learners. In addition to all this, teachers are often called upon to make appropriate choices about technology systems, resources, and services.

Applications derived from math and science help drive technology and technology returns the favor. Technology expands as mathematics and science call for more sophisticated instrumentation and techniques to study phenomena that are unobservable by other means due to danger, quantity, speed, size, or distance. As technology provides tools for investigations of the natural world, it expands mathematical and scientific knowledge beyond preset boundaries.

It is important to convey excitement about this expanding knowledge in the classroom. To do a good job of this requires that teachers use all the technological tools they can get their hands on to soften subject matter boundaries and successfully engage students in the subject they're studying. The best approach is to go beyond one-shot assignments and weave technological possibilities into the fabric of the classroom.

There is wide agreement that new technologies should be used in ways that closely correspond with practical real-world uses in order to prepare students for further education and the workplace. Technological fluency is more than a technical skill set; it involves weaving creativity and innovation into lessons, assignments, and students' lives in ways that connect to subject matter. Educators, parents, the media, and society in general are all responsible for developing the next generation of innovators. As far as the schools are concerned, if they're going "to be transformed, educational leaders need to understand and support the process of innovation."[8]

Besides altering how we learn, play, live, and work, technology has become a powerful tool for sparking students' imaginations and helping teachers teach for understanding. It can even help puncture some of the colorful balloons of mathematical nonsense, pseudoscience, and techno-trash. And, yes, computers and the Internet give students access to more people and more information. But digital tools are still "works in progress"—with changes and improvements happening at a rapid rate. So, it's important that enthusiasm not trump judgment; schools don't need expensive distractions from core instructional responsibilities.

If faith in technology simply becomes a powerful ideology, we miss an important point: technology is an important thing but not the only thing. It can be magical, but it is not the main purpose in life and it is not a silver bullet for educational improvement. When it comes to new approaches to learning with (and about) technology, a little skepticism will improve the product. Remember, although the chalkboard worked out, technological shortcuts from filmstrips to videotapes have promised a lot and delivered a lot less. Digital technology promises much more. But to paraphrase Jane Austen, "When unquestioned vanity goes to work on a weak mind it produces every kind of mischief."[9]

It is always a challenge to reorient values and priorities in a way that leads from rhetoric to a shared sense of moving toward a better reality. When it comes to motivating the innovators of the future, it requires the right mix of policy, leadership, funding, and culture. It's important to remember that, when it comes to technology, thinking about the educational process has to come first.

Before teachers can differentiate technology instruction, they have to know how to modify content, processes, and products in a way that reflects student differences. But even if teachers do a good job of filling in some of the educational potholes, a world-class school system requires a sustained societal commitment to developing an agile, smarter, and technologically savvy citizenry.

SUMMARY, CONCLUSION, AND THE WORLD OF TOMORROW

Learning with (and about) technology has a lot to do with past experiences and whether or not a student's experiential background generates possibilities for innovative behavior. At home and at school, much of what an individual learns is shaped by social interaction—including shared webs of ideas, symbols, and actions.

Innovation depends on the skill of the individual *and* the skills of the group. Continuous interaction and flexible experimentation are big difference makers. But it's not just the quality of ideas, teamwork, or new technology. Successful innovation also has a lot to do with how all the aforementioned factors interact with the world.

Like the fields of mathematics and science, progress in technology is usually incremental. Spectacular new approaches and theories are relatively rare and will continue to be so. Still, not since early man began to use tools has the human brain been affected (by technology) so quickly or so dramatically.

Change is coming on faster than ever—and it is merciless with those who aren't prepared and flexible. So, it is important to get ready for new complexities, fresh interactions, and the speed of paradigm-shifting events when they do happen. Part of getting prepared is identifying needs, asking the right questions, testing new ideas, and being aware of what's on the horizon.

Whether changes are big or small, our society will increasingly rely on innovative thinkers who can see things from a different perspective and propose imaginative solutions to problems. You can also be sure that to live, learn, and work successfully in an increasingly complex world, students, teachers, and just about everyone else must understand and make full use of technological tools. When it comes to helping students develop an imaginative understanding of technology, the key is the content of technology-related lessons and how they are connected to what is going on in the classroom.

To be useful, technology has to enhance what the teacher is trying to do, not become an annoying distraction from it. This means there are times when we have to challenge the cult of speed and turn off the intrusive array of digital devices. Still, in the hands of thoughtful and informed teachers, many technologies can be powerful levers for amplifying creativity and motivating students with a wide range of social backgrounds and individual needs (Berge and Clark, 2005).

To some extent, everyone is innovative, but there are considerable differences when it comes to creative ability and imaginative expression. What is needed is a greater emphasis on developing every child's imaginative potential. Digital technology can make an impact in the classroom by providing possibilities for collaborative activities, creative engagement, and thoughtful invention. Critical thinking and teamwork skills matter. In addition, *learning how to learn* will be an even more important skill for school and life in the twenty-first century.

In the classroom of the future, learners will be even more socially and educationally diverse than they are today. As far as instruction is concerned, teachers are bound to find themselves focusing more on how they can enhance learning for students who come from a variety of economic situations, cultures, and linguistic environments. Regardless of their background or interests, all students will need to learn how to use digital media individually and *collectively*. Such a level of technological competency involves being able to work *with* technological tools—and using those same tools to gain an *understanding* of technology.

In tomorrow's schools, the key to learning core subjects will be based on a variety of instructional models that draw upon technology, group collaboration, and positive student attitudes. As far as math, science, and technology are concerned, important goals will include generating more enthusiasm for subject matter and helping students develop competency in thoughtful problem solving.

This goes hand in hand with collaborative inquiry and using digital technology to try out new ideas. Students' creative efforts can be reinforced by formative assessment, feedback, and recognition. You can be certain that whatever unexpected events or the forces of invention bring us, fostering and accelerating innovative behavior will remain educational constants.

The crucial mechanisms for determining both individual and national success in the twenty-first century are knowledge and innovation. As far as being more precise about the nature of the future is concerned, predictions are a little like the myth that science can predict earthquakes. A lot of people are working hard to find out, but accurate predictions remain elusive. For now, the practical approach is to spend less time worrying about the unpredictable and more time preparing for the inevitable.

> The year's doors open like those of language,
> toward the unknown.
> Last night you told me:
> Tomorrow, we shall have to think up signs,
> sketch a landscape, fabricate a plan on the double edge of day and paper.
> Tomorrow, we shall have to invent, once more
> the reality of this world.
>
> —Elizabeth Bishop's translation of Octavio Paz[10]

REFERENCES

Adams, D. and Hamm, M. "Literacy, Learning, and Media." In Jason Ohler, ed., *Future Courses: A Compendium of Thought about Education, Technology, and the Future.* (Bloomington, IN: TECHNOS Press, 2001), 43–56.

Brown, H. (2007). *Knowledge and innovation: A comparative study of USA, the UK, and Japan.* New York: Routledge.

Buckingham, D. (2007). *Beyond technology: Children's learning in a digital age.* Malden, MA: Polity Press.

Burns, M. (2007). *About teaching mathematics: A K–8 resource* (3rd ed.). Sausalito, CA: Math Solutions.

Cathcart, W. G., Y. Pothier, J. Vance, and N. Bezuk. *Learning Mathematics in Elementary and Middle Schools: A Learner-Centered Approach (4th Edition)* (Upper Saddle River, NJ: Prentice Hall, 2006).

Gregory, G. H., & Chapman, C. M. (2006). *Differentiated instructional strategies: One size doesn't fit all.* Bakersfield, CA: Corwin Press.

Hamilton, B. (2007). *It's elementary! Integrating technology in the primary grades.* Eugene, OR: International Society for Technology in Education.

International Technology Education Association (ITEA). (2000). *Standards for technological literacy: Content for the study of technology.* Reston, VA: ITEA.

Kress, G. (2003). *Literacy in the new media age.* London: Routledge.

Ohler, J. (2007). *Digital storytelling in the classroom: New media pathways to literacy, learning, and creativity*. Thousand Oaks, CA: Corwin Press.

Peason, G., & Young, T. (Eds.). (2002). *Technically speaking: Why all Americans need to know more about technology*. Washington, DC: National Academy of Engineering (NAE) and National Research Council (NRC).

Ramo, J. C. (2009). *The age of the unthinkable: Why the new world disorder constantly surprises us and what we can do about it*. New York: Little, Brown, & Company.

Reys, R. E., Suydam, M. N., & Lindquist, M. M. (2004). *Helping children learn mathematics* (7th ed.). Hoboken, NJ: John Wiley & Sons.

Rose, L., & Dugger, W. (2003). ITEA/*Gallup poll reveals what Americans think about technology*. Available at http://www.iteaconnect.org/TAA/PDFs/Gallupsurvey.pdf.

Strickland, C. (2009). *Exploring differentiated instruction*. Alexandria, VA: Association for Supervision and Curriculum Development.

Wenglinsky, H. (2005). *Using technology wisely: The keys to success in schools*. New York: Teachers College Press.

Yelland, N. (2007). *Shift to the future: Rethinking learning with new technologies in education*. New York: Routledge.

Zucker. A. (2008). *Transforming schools with technology: How smart use of digital tools helps achieve six key education goals*. Cambridge, MA: Harvard Education Press.

RESOURCES AND SUGGESTED READINGS

Benjamin, A. (2005). *Differentiated instruction using technology: A guide for middle and high school teachers*. Larchmont, NY: Eye on Education.

Berge, Z., & Clark, T. (Eds.). (2005). *Virtual schools: Planning for success*. New York: Teachers College Press.

Bern, B., & Sandler, J. (2009). *Making science curriculum matter: Wisdom for the reform road ahead*. Thousand Oaks, CA: Corwin Press.

Bers, M. (2008). *Blocks to robots: Learning with technology in the early childhood classroom*. New York: Teachers College Press.

Bouerlein, M. (2008). *The dumbest generation: How the digital age stupefies young Americans and jeopardizes our future*. New York: Penguin.

Brown, S. (2009, March 23). Scott Brown on stand-up comedy: Lingua franca of the wired world. *Wired* magazine.

Evans, H. (2004). *They made America: From the steam engine to the search engine, two centuries of innovators*. New York: Little, Brown, & Company.

International Society for Technology in Education (ISTE). (2000). *National education technology for teachers*. Washington, DC: ISTE.

International Technology Education Association. (2004). *Advancing in technological literacy: Assessment, professional development, and program standards*. Reston VA: ITEA.

National Research Council. (2000). *National Science Education Standards*. Washington, DC: National Academy Press.

Parker, L. (Ed.). (2008). *Technology-mediated learning environments for young English learners: Connections in and out of school*. New York: Lawrence Erlbaum Associates.

Notes

1. David Leonhardt, "The Big Fix," *New York Times*, 27 January 2009, pg. 6, on-line edition (accessed on November 2, 2008).

CHAPTER 1

1. John Schaar, *World of Quotes*, http://www.worldofquotes.com/author/John-Schaar/1/index.html (accessed on November 10, 2008).

2. Francis Perkins, quoted in Adams S. Cohen, "Francis Perkins: Brief life of an ar-dent New Dealer: 1880–1965," *Harvard Magazine* (January-February 2009), http://harvardmagazine.com/2009/01/frances-perkins (accessed on November 15, 2008).

3. D. W. Johnson and R. T. Johnson, "Cooperation and the Use of Technology," http://www.learn-line.nrw.de/angebote/greenline/lernen/downloads/individualac-countability.pdf (accessed on November 30, 2008).

CHAPTER 2

1. George Bernard Shaw, *World of Quotes*, http://www.quotationspage.com/quote/1656.html (accessed on December 1, 2008).

2. Fareed Zakaria, from an interview on CNN, 2008.

3. "David Whyte: Preservation of the Soul," *Thinking Allowed with Dr. Jeffrey Mish-love*, video series, Thinking Aloud Production, 1988.

4. Bill Gates, quoted in Open Courseware on Critical Thinking, http://philosophy.hku.hk/think/creative/quotes.php (accessed on December 5, 2008).

5. F. Scott Fitzgerald, quoted in G. Keilor, "Petulance and the Prize," *New York Times*, 14 October 2009, online version (accessed on December 7, 2008). Originally from "The Crack Up" in *Esquire* magazine, February 1936.

6. N. Cohen, "As Data Collecting Grows, Privacy Erodes," *New York Times*, 15 February 2009, online version (accessed on December 12, 2008).

7. Tracy Kidder, *Among Schoolchildren* (Boston: Houghton Mifflin, 1989), 313.

8. Isadora Duncan, quoted in Stephen Nachmanovitch, "Bateson and the Arts," in *Kybernetes* 36, no. 7–8, (2007), 1125.

9. Marcel Proust, *The Quotations Page*, http://www.quotationspage.com/quote/31288.html (accessed on December 14, 2008).

10. George Patton, Quotes Database, http://www.quotedb.com/quotes/4112 (accessed on December 20, 2008).

11. Alfred North Whitehead, *Alfred North Whitehead, An Anthology*, eds. Mason W. Gross and F.S.C. Northrop (New York: Macmillan Press, 1953), 416.

CHAPTER 3

1. Stephen Baker, "Math Will Rock Your World," *Business Week*, 23 January 2006, p. 54.

2. Peter Abelard, quoted in Today in Science History, http://www.todayinsci.com/QuotationsCategories/T_Cat/Truth-Quotations.htm (accessed on January 15, 2009).

3. George Gordon Byron, quoted in Good Reads, http://www.goodreads.com/author/quotes/44407.George_Gordon_Byron (accessed on January 16, 2009).

4. Lady Caroline Lamb, quoted in Lady Caroline Ponsby Lamb, http://englishhistory.net/byron/lclamb.html (accessed on January 18, 2009).

5. Euripides, quoted in Quotations Book, http://quotationsbook.com/quote/28044/ (accessed on January 21, 2009).

6. Roger Bacon, quoted in Brainy Quotations, http://www.brainyquote.com/quotes/quotes/r/rogerbacon192803.html (accessed on January 23, 2009).

CHAPTER 4

1. Ian McDonald, quoted in Dave Itzkoff, "The Fuzzier Crystal Ball," *New York Times*, 23 March 2008, online version.

2. Marshall McLuhan, quoted in Paul Levinson, *Digital McLuhan: A Guide to the Information Millennium* (New York: Routledge Press, 2001), 27.

3. Voltaire, quoted in Famous Quotes, http://www.famous-quotes.net/Quote.aspx?The_perfect_is_the_enemy_of_the_good (accessed on February 18, 2009).

4. John Kenneth Galbraith, quoted in Patrick McGeehan, "Reading the Recession for Signs of the Future, *New York Times*, 12 December 2008, online version.

CHAPTER 5

1. Henry David Thoreau, quoted in Brainy Quote, http://www.brainyquote. com/quotes/quotes/h/henrydavid140556.html (accessed on April 15, 2009).

2. Bill Gates, quoted in Creative Thinking, http://philosophy.hku.hk/think/ creative/quotes.php (accessed on April 18, 2009).

3. G. K. Chesterton, quoted in Think Exist, http://thinkexist.com/quotation/ education_is_simply_the_soul_of_a_society_as_it/206678.html (accessed on April 25, 2009).

4. Leo Bogart, *The Age of Television: A Study of Viewing Habits and the Impact of Television on American Life* (New York: Fredrick Unger Publishing, 1956), pg #.

5. T. S. Eliot, "Burnt Norton" from Four Quartets, quoted in Athenaeum Reading Room, http://evans-experientialism.freewebspace.com/eliot_burnt_norton.htm (accessed on May 15, 2009).

6. John Dewey, "My Pedagogic Creed," quoted in Philosophy for Children, http://www.childrenphilosophy.com/dewey.htm (accessed on May 18, 2009).

7. Joshua Cooper Ramo, *The Age of the Unthinkable: Why the New World Disorder Constantly Surprises Us and What We Can Do about It* (New York: Little, Brown and Co., 2009), 240.

8. Andy Zucker, "The Role of Nonprofits in Educational Technology Innovation," A Concord Consortium White Paper (December 2007), p. 1. Available online, http://www.concord.org/publications/detail/2007-CC-nonprofits-white-paper.pdf.

9. Jane Austen, quoted in D. Adams and M. Hamm, *Literacy Today: New Standards Across the Curriculum* (New York: RoutledgeFalmer, 1999), 185. Original quote paraphrased, Jane Austen's *Emma*.

10. Octavio Paz, trans. Elizabeth Bishop, quoted in M. Greene, "Public Spaces in Local Places," *Phenomenology + Pedagogy* 10 (2002), 243–251.

About the Authors

Dennis Adams (Ph.D.) is a Canadian educational consultant who has taught classes at McGill University in Montreal. He is author of more than twelve books and a hundred journal articles on various educational topics.

Mary Hamm is a professor at San Francisco State University. Her specialties are science and mathematics. She has worked on both science and math standards project and has published more than ten books and eighty journal articles on these topics.

Breinigsville, PA USA
29 January 2010
231585BV00002B/3/P